Yukoners
True Tales Of The Yukon

by H. Gordon-Cooper

Riverrun Publishing • **Vancouver**

Dedicated
*to the memory of the late
Ira VanBibber
a Yukoner in the best tradition
and the greatest of story tellers.*

Yukoners
True Tales Of The Yukon

Acknowledgments: I wish to thank Ethel Wright who first typed the original MS. *YUKONERS* was first published in a 15-part serialization in *The Whitehorse Star*, in 1974. An editor with *The Whitehorse Star*, Jim Bebe, offered his kind but firm suggestions which were incorporated into the articles. Gratitude also goes out to Margaret Ford who typed and edited a subsequent MS. For her careful attention to salient details in the final proofreading and copy-editing I wish to thank Laurie Arber.

Cataloguing In Publication Data

Gordon-Cooper, H.
Yukoners

  ISBN 0-920690-00-9 cloth bound
  ISBN 0-920690-02-5 paperback

1. Yukon Territory — Biography. 2. Pioneers —
Yukon Territory — Biography. I. Title.
FC4005.G6 971.9'1'020922 C78-002121-5
F1093.G67

graphic design and production: interface
illustrations: June Foote
cartography: Linda Taylor
fotografics: Norm Brandel

Riverrun Publishing,
P.O. Box 4915, Main Station,
Vancouver, B.C., Canada
Telephone: (604) 688-1760

Printed in Canada
by
Friesen Printers
Altona, Manitoba
R0G 0B0

Foreword

*In a land such as the Yukon, with its colourful
past matched by its colourful characters, tales
abound of the perils and adventures experienced by
those hardy sourdoughs who first pioneered the
country. Many are the tales that have been told in
the still of the unequalled splendor of a Yukon
evening while gathered around the campfire with
close companions. Yarn swapping is indeed a
Yukon staple. I am one of those who deem it a
privilege to know the author of the stories in this
book. In setting them down here he has maintained
his skill as a narrator. I have often had the pleasure
of experiencing this on camping forays with him;
but, even more important, by doing so he is
preserving a part of our history and the memory of
those about whom he writes for future Yukoners.*

Erik Nielsen, D.F.C., Q.C.
M.P. for the Yukon Territory

Fred Guder and the grizzly (see page 113)

Author's Introduction

A group of men were sitting in the smoking compartment of a cross-Canada train, when the compartment was entered by another man who looked around and asked if there was anybody in the group from the Yukon.

"I am," said one of the men.

"Good," said the newcomer: "lend me your bottle opener, will you please."

It may be the harshness, at times, or the length of the winters or any number of other indeterminate factors that make Yukoners different, and that difference so appreciated by other Yukoners. And so it is with those of us who spend our lives in the high northwest.

All these yarns have to do with men of the north. The stories are true and, with the exception of one or two, most of the personalities are still alive.

It is to be hoped that our stories will prove to be interesting and entertaining.

The pity of it is that they cannot be listened to over steaming hot rums on cold winter nights, rather than read from a book.

H. Gordon-Cooper
Whitehorse, Y.T.
July 3rd, 1978.

Gunfight At Sulphur Creek

"Cam" Cameron

Gunfight at
Sulphur Creek

Corporal G.I. Cameron I/C Royal Canadian Mounted Police, circa 1945.

In these latitudes, north of '60, the operation of a bush flying service in the winter time presents many problems; among them are the short days and at times the extreme cold.

It had been dull and overcast, with the temperature around 25 below. It was getting close to the time of day when fliers do not go anywhere because of the necessity of having to stay overnight. Staying overnight is fine in the summertime, but during the winter away from base there are none of the amenities to simplify the business of getting an aircraft warmed up and ready for flight the next day.

In actual fact, it is possible to get an aircraft into the air in cold weather, but it is a laborious business and it was the custom to avoid having to do it if it was at all possible.

At 3:00 p.m. the Indian Agent phoned requesting a trip to Fort Selkirk, 150 miles down the river.

An Indian woman there, the day after having delivered her baby, had sat up quickly during some excitement or other in the cabin and had contracted a severe sustaining pain. Would we bring her to town immediately, taking some pills along to give her in the meantime?

During the winter time the people that live down the Yukon River were virtually locked in until spring when the ice goes out and the river boats could navigate again. The term or expression "going outside", which means going south for the winter or during the winter, is still used rather glibly here in the north, when in actual fact it does not really apply anymore. Before the roads and highways were built, a bush flying operation was the only physical contact these people had with the "outside" once the rivers were frozen. It is true most of them kept dogs for communication amongst themselves and the various communities were linked with well-used sleigh trails. Now there was an aircraft service available, however, nobody would contemplate a 150 mile trip with dogs, especially with a sick person along and the inevitable possibility of having to break trail at least from Carmacks to Whitehorse, a distance of 100 miles.

We held the mail contract between Whitehorse, Carmacks, Minto and Fort Selkirk. We brought the people their mail, sometimes did their shopping, brought out their Christmas liquor, hauled them back and forth when they were ill, and generally considered them to be our responsibility.

Here was an emergency! The doctor said he preferred to have the Indian woman brought in rather than make the trip himself. I left at 3:30 in the afternoon to do one and a half hours of flying in one hour of daylight.

I reached Carmacks one hour later, although it was now dark, I was out of the woods, so to speak, for there was the Yukon River to follow for the last 50 miles of the trip.

Corporal Cameron of the Mounted Police was waiting with a flashlight at the edge of the clearing, and I taxied for his light when I got down. With his aid I soon found the opening and the road, and taxied a quarter of a mile back to the river and the village. I gave Mrs. Cameron the pills, drained the oil from the engine into an open four gallon blazo tin, put it on the front seat, put the nose tent on the engine, the skis on sticks, tied down the wings, and Cam and I headed for some warmth and some supper.

There is nothing to equal the warmth and comfort that seems to exude from a good wood fire in a heater and so, following supper, we settled down in Cam's sturdy log dwelling to drink a steaming hot rum and yarn a little.

"That must be a little dangerous making a landing when it's dark like that", Cam observed.

"Well", I said, "the field is wide and fairly long, and being close to the river it's easy enough to find. It shows up white among the dark trees, as does the river which I followed from Carmacks. It's just a matter of motoring down until the skis touch. I was certainly glad to see your light at the edge of the clearing, because I could not for the life of me see where the opening was for the road to the river. I don't mind something like that because it's easy to cope with. It's made easy by the fact that the opposing forces are static. That is to say, you have control of your aircraft and the field is not going to move away and land you in the trees. There are things that could happen, to be sure, but nothing that you do not bring about yourself. And so, with training and experience you avoid the difficulties. If you were able to stand still—nothing would happen.

"Suppose, for instance, you were pitting your hunting skill against a grizzly bear who knows you are there, or if, on the other hand, you are having a fight with another man—you must figure out your moves and those of the opposite side as well, because they are not static by any means. What would happen if you stood still then?"

"I suppose that is largely true", Cam mused, "but I remember an instance some years ago when I stood still during a gun fight—not having any choice in the matter—and the opposing force or other side as you call it, was about to go into action, when a third force came between me and my certain death in a very fortuitous manner. Call it a third force if you like. Call it anything you like. It is the sort of happening that is beyond our understanding. I cannot help thinking, however, that I must have been in rhythm with the cosmos and that my appointed time had not yet come.

"It happened in the Dawson area a few years ago, 1927 to be exact, during the month of January.

"In those days there were perhaps 30 or 40 of us policing the Territory, and I should think about 15 actually in the division at Dawson.

"In any case Sergeant/Major Dan McLean called me in first thing in the morning and instructed me to take Constable Sonnie, the teamster, and Constable Bob Scafe on a patrol to Sulphur Creek and take whatever action was thought to be necessary. He explained further that Constable Burt at Granville had phoned in to report that an old miner called Smith had slipped a cog and taken a shot at a neighbour with a rifle—a fellow called Scotty Low, who ran the roadhouse. Nobody knows why he did this, and Scotty told us later that from what he knew of him he was supposed to have been an old gunman from down Texas way. It seems there have been no end of mad trappers in this northland of ours, and the oldsters are full of tales concerning them, some of which contain elements of truth.

"The three of us set out as soon as possible with a team of horses and a sleigh, and travelled all day. From Dawson we headed south over the long rows of tailings in the Klondike Valley about ten miles to Hunker Creek. Up Hunker some fifteen miles to the summit where roads lead to such other fabulously rich creeks as Dominion, Granville, Quartz, all leading away from King Solomon's Dome. In this instance, we swung right, down Green Gulch to Sulphur Creek, about 30 or 40 miles from Dawson.

"Each creek had its little settlement usually consisting of a road house, a mining recorder, miners' cabins and an R.C.M.P. constable at one of the camps in the area. The camps were usually located at the discovery claim on each creek, and the subsequent claims then became known as Nos. 1, 2, 3, etc., either above or below discovery.

"We arrived at 10:00 or 11:00 p.m. at Sulphur Creek. It was a cold, clear, moonlight night, the sky was full of northern lights, and we passed Smith's place on the way to the roadhouse where Constable Burt was waiting for us. Constable Burt warned us that the man meant business, and that there was certain to be trouble. We put the horses away, had a bite to eat, and talked the situation over while we warmed up.

"It was decided we should attend to the matter without further ado; Burt and Scafe were to go to the front while Sonnie and myself were to circle to the rear of the cabin. It was an old log cabin about 16 by 20 feet with a door on the right and a window on the left in front. There was a lean-to at the back, or an overhang, where he had his wood piled, and there was of course a passage between the wood and the cabin wall to the back door.

"Burt had previously made an endeavour to reason with the old chap, but had been driven from the place with a gun, and as a consequence they approached the front to the side of the door and called for him to come out. He yelled for them to beat it, and fired through the door. By this time Sonnie and myself had circled to the back, and as the two others started around to join us and we were about to rush the back door, he beat us to it and came out with a barrage of rapid fire from behind his wood pile.

14

"We returned his fire, but as he was running back and forth in the dark behind his wood pile we could not see him, and as we were out in the moonlight we hit the deep snow and he had us effectively pinned down.

"It was cold—about 40 below—and although we were warmly dressed we had left our parkas back at the roadhouse as, naturally, we had not anticipated any such caper as this.

"We were there for possibly an hour exchanging spasmodic fire, and then I remembered that Constable Sonnie was some distance off to my right. Try as I might I could not see him. When I returned my attention to the cabin, the old chap had come out from behind his wood pile and was coming straight for me. By that time we were too cold to move with any speed, but I got to one knee, and as I could not squeeze the trigger of my revolver with one hand I managed to get a shot away using both hands. Of course it missed, but it made him drop into the snow. The next thing I saw, he was standing up again and pointing his rifle straight at my head.

"You may recall having read or heard of men facing the immediate prospect of certain death and how, in the split second, it is said their lives pass in review in their minds. No such thing happened to me. I recall only that I was completely paralyzed, and waited for him to pull the trigger—which he did. There was a terrific report and a flash—he looked with some amazement at the end of his gun—turned and belted for his wood pile with more alacrity than I would have thought possible.

"It was apparent then that he had plugged his rifle barrel with snow and blown the end off it.

"I became conscious again of the extreme cold, and as I knew the others to be in a like state we withdrew one at a time under cover of each other's fire, and got back to the roadhouse to thaw out.

"I can appreciate now how wonderful it must be to be rescued at sea dying of thirst, or come in off a desert parched and dehydrated, and be given a long, cool drink of life-saving water. You can imagine how grateful we were to get out of the position we had been in, and get into a warm room again. For my part, I was grateful to be there at all!

"Well, there you are. How does that fit into your proposition that there are two forces, yours and the opposing force?" Cam was laughing. "There I was standing, or kneeling still if you like, unable to move, and I knew for certain what the opposing force was going to do and that it would mean curtains for me without a doubt. I knew what he was going to do and so did he, and he did it. So, there you have a third force that had made other arrangements than the one we had contemplated."

"In any case, Cam, what happened then?"

"We posted a guard", he went on, "which was changed every two hours, in a position that commanded a good view of the cabin and the surrounding area, and sent Constable Sonnie to Granville to phone and report the situation, as it was a little out of the ordinary. He returned subsequently with instructions to withold any further action, and that the O.C. was sending out Inspector Humby, Sergeant/Major Dan McLean, Sergeant Jerry Daley and Constable Cruikshanks, and that they were leaving immediately. They arrived the following night after dark and brought more ammunition, medical supplies, and gear.

"It had been a beautiful day all day, cold, crisp and clear, and we had called many times and had never received any response. During the morning an old timer, known as Swift, who at one time had worked for Swift's Packing House, came to the roadhouse with his old 45/70 black powder blunderbuss and offered to help us "smoke him out". He said he "never did like the son-of-a-bitch anyway". It's funny how these old fellows seem to get a kick out of a good scrap. We thanked him for his offer of assistance, of course, but had to explain that this was a police matter, and that we could not under any circumstances permit him to take part.

"Later in the day Smith came cautiously out with his rifle in his hand and a pail for snow. When we called to him he dropped the pail, fired, and ran in again. Well, to make a long story short, when the second party arrived the following day, we deployed around the cabin and made further attempts to reason with the old fellow, but all we got was a flurry of rifle fire, which we returned. Toward noon, under cover of fire from above, three of us rushed the cabin and found him dead.

"Everything in the cabin was shot to pieces. He had barricaded the door with table and chairs, and behind this he had shot guns, knives and a second rifle all laid out ready for use. If, when we had made the cabin, he had still been alive, he would have made it hot for us, and would have nailed one or two of us for certain.

"We brought him back to Dawson in the sleigh, and after a coroner's hearing he was buried in the old cemetery."

I asked Cam how it was possible to bury people in the dead of winter when the ground is frozen solid. "Nothing to it", he said. He contemplated his mug with a very serious face. "We generally leave them out by the wood pile until they are frozen good and solid. Then in the spring when the ground softens up a little, we sharpen their feet and drive them in."

Such a man was Corporal Cameron.

Last Days
of
Orloff King

Last Days of Orloff King

Dam, spillway, and automatic trip gate similar to the one used by Orloff King on his placer claim on Nansen Creek, 30 miles west of Carmacks.

There is a green slope on a high ridge of hills some thirty miles west of the village of Carmacks that looks down past a log cabin, a tool shed, a cache, and a privy. At the bottom of the slope flows a creek on which has been built a dam and a spillway of rough lumber.

In the spring and early summer, when the melting snows bring life to the creek, the dam holds back the water in a reservoir. When the level of the water rises, a float trips a gate and the water bursts free, washing as it goes, the earth from the sides of the creek. The water, discoloured from the yellow earth of the banks, rushes and washes down the creek bottom carrying with it earth, gravel and stones. Once more the gate falls, holding back the creek and the cycle begins again.

The man who built this dam and spillway was Orloff King, and he had rigged it so that the earth from the sides of the creek would wash down in such a fashion that the gold in the gravel would wash out and be left in the natural riffles made by the rough surface of the creek bed. Periodically he would push more dirt down from the eroded banks and into its natural sluice box. Soon the time would come when the banks of the stream were too far from the water and then he would move his dam and spillway farther upstream.

Before the move, however, it was time for what is known as a clean-up when he gathered the black sand and heavier materials from the bottom of the creek and recovered the gold from these deposits with the aid of his gold pan and a little mercury.

The process was quite simple, and he could do it in his cabin using a wash tub full of water, or do it right in the creek.

His gold pan was roughly the size of a good wash basin and about as deep, except that the bottom was flat and the sides sloped out to a greater extent. When he bought it new it was a bright shiny metal so he put it on the fire to blue it. By making the bottom blue it is easier to see tiny specks of gold as they trail along behind the black sand under the effluence of the swirling water.

A placer man can tell by the size of his pan the number of pans to one cubic yard of dirt and he is able to gauge the value of his ground as so much per yard according to how much value there is in one pan or an average of several pans.

He heaps up the pan with the material to be washed and immerses it in the water where it is agitated and washed. The cleaned, coarse gravel is scooped off the top. Eventually through a process of dipping and swirling the coarser material, which rises to the top, is washed out over the edge of the pan, and there is nothing left but the heavier black sand and any gold.

If the gold is coarse it is easy to get it completely clear of sand, but if it is very fine a little quick silver is added to the sand because it has an affinity for the gold. The quick silver soon picks it all up and leaves the sand. This quick silver is then squeezed through a wet chamois and what remains is a spongy ball composed of gold dust and quick silver.

The remainder of the quick silver in the ball is removed with heat, as it vaporizes readily, but great care must be taken not to breathe the fumes which are poisonous. The quick silver can be recovered by condensation but is usually such a small amount that it is simply burned off. The safest way is to put the ball on a small shovel, open the front of the stove and hold it in over the fire so that the fumes are carried up the chimney by the draft. What remains is a porous ball of gold.

Orloff didn't get rich from his claim but he made a little and he was fond of the green slope, the splashing creek, the clear cool air, and his sturdy log cabin. The gophers that burrowed under his cabin were his pets, but mostly he enjoyed the quiet and the solitude.

He certainly wasn't rich in a material way but in other respects he could well have been considered a wealthy man.

He took his place among men easily and with harmony and always enjoyed the highest regard of his friends. Many men, enmeshed in the tumble and the turmoil of a different life, would have envied the easy pace, the quiet and peacefulness of such a life as his.

He was an old Yukoner. For some years he had trapped along the winding river in the Nordenskihold Valley where he made a good living from his furs. And then as he grew older and his aging frame objected more and more to the long trapline trails carrying a heavy pack, he turned his endeavours to the more leisurely life he had led for the past fifteen years, on his claims along the ridge above Nansen Creek.

He was a veteran of the Spanish American war and drew a pension, which, now that his vigour was failing, kept him comfortably supplied with his simple needs without too much exertion.

He had two neighbours in the area, each occupied with the same endeavours and each situated on a different creek. The three of them, all old timers, often visited together and usually spent their time telling each other how to run a placer mine. Mostly they spent their winters in Carmacks, returning in the spring to their creeks where they stayed until the following fall.

Gordon Dickson was a younger man and although he was not strictly a neighbour, since he made his headquarters at Nansen Creek, he wandered the surrounding country prospecting and always stopped in for a word with Orloff when he was in the vicinity. The two men enjoyed each other's company and the older man would bring out a jug of lowbush cranberry wine to enhance the pleasure of his friend's visit. He seldom drank the wine himself because he had an ulcerated stomach. He made it to serve his friends when they dropped in on periodical visits.

During the winter months Orloff flew back and forth between Carmacks and Whitehorse as it pleased his fancy and it was while flying him back and forth on these trips that I came to know him so well. He was exceptionally good company and we had many laughs together and many a chew of tobacco. Whenever we met, the first thing that he did was produce a jackknife and a plug of tobacco.

I had flown him to Nansen Creek that spring along with his grub, some gear, and heavy radio batteries. His interest in world affairs, the latest tunes, and particularly the world series ball games made his radio a valued piece of equipment. We piled the stuff at the end of the flight strip—spuds, flour, sugar, etc., and twelve tins of tobacco. It was six miles up over the ridge to his cabin and he figured to pack the stuff in with six easy trips. He had lots of time, so he said. He paid me his fare, passed his knife and plug of tobacco, and I was ready to be off.

"Well, I'm on my own now, see you in the fall", he said.

I remember that an odd inexplicable feeling came over me and we both looked away as I shook his hand and said good-bye. Just a fleeting sensation of uneasiness which was gone and forgotten the minute I waved a final cheerio and taxied around for a take-off. That was the last time I was to see him alive.

Several months later a wireless message was received asking for an aircraft to pick up two passengers at Carmacks for Nansen Creek. It was late in the afternoon when I landed in Carmacks and found my friends, Corporal Cameron from the Royal Canadian Mounted Police Post at Selkirk and Gordon Dickson, waiting at the end of the strip. I particularly remember Gordon's appearance at the time; he had been in the bush for a whole year. The elbows and knees of his clothes had been neatly patched using white string for thread, and he wore a good foot of heavy red-brown beard. He is a good sized man and rugged and he had a suggestion of the freshness of wild animals about him.

They told me the news that Orloff King was dead.

Gordon had left him in his cabin the night before and walked out 37 miles to Carmacks during the night and morning.

Corporal Cameron, on river patrol at the time, happened to be in Carmacks. He was an older man than Gordon, but equally as rugged, and his years in the north had lent him a quiet dignity. "Cam" was a man who knew and understood life in the north. This was to be, by no means, the first time he had laid to rest one of his old friends.

In these years there were still many old timers living out the last of their allotted time, as was their want, in their cabins on the creeks and along the rivers. Solitary men who had been trappers, woodcutters for the river boats, or who had just found themselves left over from the days of the gold rush in '98. Most of them had lived by themselves for the greater part of their lives and there would seem to be no good reason for changing now.

By and large they were fine old men, who kept their places tidy, their saws and axes sharp and busied themselves with day to day living, enjoying peace and solitude while they patiently waited for their time to run out ·

Cam told us of one old timer who met him with a smile and a waggle of his head each time he came by. "Not yet, Cam", he would say, "Not this time. But when the time comes, plant me over there in the sun beside that tree within sight of the river. I've watched those river boats go by for quite a few years". And sure enough when the time finally came, that is where Cam, with respect and dignity, would bury him.

We took off from Carmacks immediately, landing at the flight strip below Nansen Creek just at dark, and hiked together three miles to the old camp site where Gordon had his headquarters. We decided to spend the night, as we were not anxious to travel a further three miles in the dark any more than we were anxious to arrive at the dead man's cabin in the middle of the night. We cooked up a supper and decided to set out again after a sleep. Following supper, as we relaxed in the warm cabin, Gordon told us of Orloff's passing.

He had been in the habit of dropping by to see Orloff every three or four weeks and this particular time he'd arrived just at dusk to find Orloff in his bunk, in a cold cabin, quite sick and very weak. He was glad he had dropped in when he found his old friend in this condition, but he was not half as glad as Orloff was to see him.

"I have been trying to die for the last three nights", Orloff told him, "and I can't make it."

His stomach had been bothering him, and he had developed a hemorrhage that had brought him to his weakened condition, and he felt that his time had come. Lying alone in his cheerless cabin he had given considerable thought, probably for the first time, to matters relating to what he would find when he came to the end of his time here. First he had written in the margin of a magazine, "Give my claims to my sister Lottie", and he had noted her address as somewhere in the United States, and he had signed it. Then he settled down to try to figure out what he could from the pages of an old prayer book that he had among his possessions for years. The prospect of leaving this life for a possible other one, about which he knew nothing but a vague series of conflicting opinions, had caused him at that point a great deal of concern.

Now, however, he had some company; somebody with whom to talk. The lamp and the cheerful fire had been lit, he had eaten a bowl of hot soup, and he had livened up considerably. He explained how relieved he was now that someone had come.

He sat up and, dangling his legs over the edge of the bunk, he fell to talking. He had been very despondent. Apart from the physical discomfort he had been enduring, he could not reconcile the idea of not knowing what was likely to happen.

For awhile they spoke of trivial things; his pet gophers that burrowed beneath the cabin; and he laughed at the rum methods employed by his neighbours to recover the gold from their creeks. He had perked up to such an extent that Gordon could not help thinking that all he had needed was company, and that he would be well again in a short while.

Following a long silence, the old man asked him abruptly what he figured his chances would be if there was a life after death, and what he figured he would find there.

To a young man such as Gordon Dickson, used to a rough and ready existence and not given particularly to serious thought, this, as can be seen, was quite a question, especially coming from the lips of his friend who could so easily be on the brink of taking such a trip.

Nothing but a good answer would do, and he could tell from the genuine anxiety registered on Orloff's face that he did require some answer. He thought for a long time before he gave Orloff the answer he was sitting waiting for.

"Orloff", he said, "millions of people have died during the span of your life on this earth. Millions will still die after you have gone, and you will have known many of these people at some time or another. It seems to me that if you have been able to hit a pretty good average here on earth, you should do just as well when you get to the other side. I guess you will be among the same people."

"And", he added, "being an old Yukoner you should have a little edge on most of them!"

For a long time the old man sat thoughtfully, but he appeared to be satisfied, for the troubled look had left his face, and his young friend's last remark had brought a smile to his eyes. Finally he moved his feet back up on the bunk and pulled up his sleeping bag.

"Guess I'll have a little sleep", he said.

For a time he lay on his back breathing easily, while the younger man sat on the other side of the cabin near the stove and read a magazine. Once he looked across as Orloff, breathing heavily once or twice, rolled over on his side. When the story was finished Gordon laid aside his magazine and going across to the bunk, found that Orloff had indeed breathed his last.

He had made it this time. It seemed that all he had needed was not to have to do it alone. He had eaten a warm comforting meal. There was a light and a good fire in his cabin, and a friend by his side. But most important of all, he had been able to see reason in the assurance that everything was going to be all right. He had set out on his strange journey with as little concern as though he had gone down to the creek for a pail of water.

We arrived at the cabin on the green slope at 5:30 a.m. The sun had been up for an hour or so, but the leaves of the buck brush were still wet with a heavy dew. Gordon and I dug his grave while Cam arranged the effects in his cabin and made out his report.

Before we carried him from the cabin, wrapped in his sleeping bag and bound around with a rope, we filled three mugs with low bush cranberry wine. We held them up together and drank to his memory, and we wished that our friend, Orloff King, had found things to his liking.

We buried him on the green slope in the warm morning sunshine, looking down past the buildings to the dam and the spillway on the creek.

A Troubled
Mercy Flight

Harry Gordon-Cooper

A Troubled Mercy Flight

A Yukon scene in early fall.

Sometimes it becomes barely possible to be anything but an out-and-out fatalist when considering the turn of events over a given period. The number of things that happen, the formidable obstacles that seem to be strategically placed which require surmounting, all tend to impress upon the interesting possibility of some sort of a force arranging things in order to provide itself with entertainment and amusement as it contemplates our efforts, both good and bad.

The pride and joy of our bush flying service was a "Sea-Bee", an amphibious aircraft that flew from and alighted on both land and water. It was a wonderful aircraft, and we were particularly attached to it. The registration was CF—FOW.

Our Sea-Bee was equipped with a Franklin 315 horsepower engine, a Hartnel variable-pitch propeller, that could be swung through to reverse. Wheels that could be left on or removed with ease because the hydraulic brakeline had press-and-snap fittings that did not require the use of wrenchs, etc. In the winter we operated it on skis, which in itself was remarkable.

There were many features that made the Sea-Bee an excellent aircraft for a bush operation, features that far outweighed some of the disadvantages.

With a conventional float plane, a pilot on a river by himself or with his passengers on board needs to untie, push off and jump aboard, all in the expectation that the engine will start immediately. If it does not, then both he and his aircraft are in trouble and in danger, completely at the mercy of the wind and the current as they float down stream without any means of control.

If there is somebody to cast off for him after he has the engine started, he must die a thousand deaths lest they walk into the propeller, which cannot be seen; and he knows that this has happened many times.

On the Sea-Bee the propeller is high up at the back, a pusher, and is out of the way of people stepping into the plane. The nose door is used for loading at the front. When all are aboard, start it with the nose pushing into the bank—warm up, run up, then put the propeller into reverse, back out and away without any problems. But—to our story.

It was fall. The whole country was ablaze with color, and soon the rivers would be throwing ice and flying with the water-borne aircraft would be at an end for the season.

We were taking a party to Fairweather Lake about 150 miles due east of Mayo. Four men and their grub and gear. Two trips from Mayo. The first trip—the engineer and an Indian helper, and of course their immediate requirements in food and gear. The second trip would be the old prospector whose ground was being examined, and a young student engineer whose name was Jones.

From Mayo we followed the Stewart River east until we saw the canyons and the rapids of the Hess River. We swung onto the Hess and followed through a long stretch of beautiful country, along and around a bend to Fairweather Lake. Before landing we circled a couple of times to enable the engineer to select the best place to be put on the shore line.

Up to this point everything was fine. Warm clear weather, and Jack Frost had certainly been busy with his paint brush. It is such a delight to fly in these conditions. We landed on the water, taxied in to the selected shore line, unloaded and pushed off again onto the calm waters of the lake.

It must have been at this point that mischief makers were about to start their depredations, for the motor would not start.

When you are out 150 miles from anywhere, it certainly is not in your best interest to sit and turn the motor over until there is no more battery. Something was obviously wrong and must be corrected. Accordingly, I climbed out and up on the wing, removed the engine cowling and backed out one of the spark plugs—which I dropped!

While I watched, fascinated and horrified it rolled along the wing root, down over the edge, bounced on the hull and rolled to a stop against the protruding edge of the deck.

This was a time when in a split second your mind pictures all the results of having done such a ridiculous thing at this time and place. I could picture the second aircraft arriving in a couple of days—our competitor, as we have no other aircraft that will operate off the water—and finding everything just dandy except for the fact that I had dropped one of the aircraft's spark plugs into the lake. Now he must return for another spark plug, and the costs mount steadily. Even yet the thought brings on illness.

But there is the spark plug safe and sound, and upon being rescued is put immediately back where it belongs and, wonder of wonders, the motor starts.

"Well, that was pretty lucky to get out of that one", but maybe this was just an indicator—what is next?

When this sort of thing starts, I generally figure now is the time to be more careful than ever, not only about doing something foolish—as I had just been guilty of—but about everything—everything. And for awhile this is what is done. The fiendish part about it is, however, that you are given just the right amount of time to become complacent and—bang!—here we go again! We didn't have to wait long.

I must concede to the powers that arranged this caper—that we were not put to too much of a danger or disadvantage. It was, as has been noted, a fine, warm, sunny day; and we were over a flat, wide, slow-moving stretch of the river when my eye caught the movement of two needles on the instrument panel. The oil pressure guage and the oil temperature gauge indicator needles both went "off the clock" at the same time, right to the post.

The engine didn't miss a beat, and had the instruments not been noticed it could have conceivably gone merrily along to the point where it would seize up and we could have been over the Hess Canyon and rapids.

I throttled back and subsequently turned the engine off, and we sat down comfortably on the broad smooth surface of the Stewart River. It was necessary to start the engine again and run it for the space of time it took us to get to the shore, but it suffered no damage from this.

When we climbed out at the river bank we found the tail assembly and most of the rest of the aircraft back of the engine coated with crankcase oil, and it was discovered that the oil cooling radiator had burst.

It was decided then that the older man should stay in comfort at the aircraft. He had his sleeping bag and food and whatever else he needed; and that Jones and I would head down the river for Mayo.

Accordingly we made up some packs, took a small axe and a gun, and set off. I should think it took us half an hour to decide that travelling through that type of country certainly was not meant to be done on foot. Had we been able to find a trail, and there undoubtedly was one or several, then it would not have been quite so bad. We turned back after deciding to make a raft and travel by water.

Aboard the aircraft were twelve spikes, a small coil of haywire, such as is made up by the Hudson Bay Company for trappers, a good length of cotton clothes line; and with this we had a good raft put together in short order. We each had a long pole, a block to sit on, and a joint pile of sticks and branches to keep our stuff out of the water.

Between where we landed and Mayo, the Stewart meanders down the floor of the valley, taking its time and following such a twisted course that it probably only goes one mile for every four that it moves.

Our progress was slow, but it was infinitely better than a struggling through fifty miles of bush. When we got hungry we poled to the river bank, picked up some flat rocks and a supply of wood, made our fire on the rocks in the centre of the raft, and got under way again without losing too much time.

The surface of the river was sprinkled with yellow autumn leaves, and although the river bank was going slowly by, it was brought home to us that we were not travelling through the water as one does in a boat or some kind of craft, but just idling along on the water and with it. The leaves that we found ourselves among stayed with us with slight variations in position, all the way down.

We warmed up some beans and made a billy can of tea, and with this we refreshed ourselves as we dried our socks by the fire and made a leisurely way towards Mayo. All in all, it was pleasant enough.

As the day wore on we came upon a boom of logs made fast to the river bank. A logging operation. The men had a fast river boat, and for $25.00 took us on to Mayo forthwith, where, after phoning Whitehorse, we stayed over night at the old Silver Inn.

The situation was becoming a little complicated now. We had two men at Fairweather Lake, one man partly there in an unserviceable aircraft, and one man and the pilot in Mayo.

We had another oil cooler for the aircraft, but it was one that had been replaced because it had become a little plugged and kept the oil pressure unnecessarily high. It was decided that the other pilot, Bud Harbottle, would bring this old cooler and some oil to Mayo in the Piper Super Cruiser;and the boatman had agreed to wait over and carry us back up river to the aircraft. We would be mobile again towards the close of the following day. The old oil cooler would suffice to get the aircraft back to base, where a new cooler freshly ordered would be installed.

The oil cooler looks exactly like a small radiator from a motor car. It is mounted over the engine, and has an air impeller in front of it to carry the heat away as the oil circulates through.

Our old friend, the prospector, was in good shape when we got back, and happy to see us again so soon. I noticed, though that the hull of the aircraft was extremely low in the water and realized that she never sits in the water for any length of time, and that a small leak in the hull would not show up until this happened.

Once the alternate cooler was installed and a supply of new oil poured in, it was a short distance back to Mayo.

After due consideration, it was decided that in the circumstances we should request our competitor to finish the charter for us, as it was felt our aeroplane, while still able to fly, was not really in first class condition without a new cooler, and that I should bring it back to base. Back at Mayo, by chance, we found Herman Peterson with his Fairchild 71 on floats, and he agreed happily to finish the work for us. Normally he is based at Atlin, down in B.C.

It is odd that I did not realize now that trouble was only just starting. In the back of my mind was the thought that we would have the Sea-Bee back at base in a few hours, and I was relieved by the decision not to finish the charter with an indifferent serviceability for the aircraft. I saw no objection, however, to complying with the request of a gentleman and his wife to be flown from Mayo to Minto on the Yukon River, as it was almost on the way in any case.

The following day then, after getting my two former passengers and their gear into Herman's aircraft and seeing them off, we repaired to the airport to set off in the Sea-Bee for Minto.

Eventually we were fuelled, loaded, started and warmed up, and got under way for Minto. The air was cold, and as we climbed higher the inside of the windows began to fog up and then to freeze. I switched on the small rubber-bladed fan that was mounted in a position to blow air on the front window. It started and then stopped, so we continued on with no vision except out the side. My side window I could keep clear because I could reach it.

The route from Mayo to Minto I was familiar with, so it presented no hazard, even flying half blind. Soon, however, we flew into warmer air so that the difficulty resolved itself.

In the meantime, the thing that did constitute a hazard was my friend's requirement to get rid of some of the liquid he had taken on in the shape of beer at Mayo before leaving. He and his wife, of course, were sitting in the back seat, as the plane trimmed better when as much of the weight as possible was towards the back.

Normally we carried containers for the use of passengers who became air sick; but today there was no container of any description that would have been suitable for this purpose.

He had a bag containing half a dozen beer so he decided to drink one of these and then he would have an empty bottle to use—and this he did.

It is difficult to describe the antics a man goes through in order to position himself in a confined space so as to be able to use a beer bottle for the purpose my friend had in mind. Whatever he had to do, in any case, his wife found to be objectionable, and so she decided to climb over into the front seat, complaining that she was in an unhappy situation.

A pilot flying half blind is hazard enough and the situation was not improved by my friend's difficulty, or the difficulty his wife was having to get herself over into the front seat. She was compelled to expose a length of nylon-covered leg and sundry feminine dainties, so that any pilot would have found himself hard put to pay attention to his flying. We all had a good laugh in any case, and arrived in Minto without mishap.

At Minto I was handed a wireless message that had been relayed from Mayo. It directed me to stop at Ole Wickstrom's wood camp and bring to Whitehorse a young and very ill Indian woman. She had a three day old child, and was beset with septic complications.

I was at a loss to understand the reasons behind asking me to do this, when it was known that my aircraft was indifferently serviceable, and to carry a very sick person as well. It was subsequently learned that there was no other means available to bring this person in, and there was certainly come urgency inherent in the request.

As it was, George Milne of Whitehorse Flying Services, our competitor, was on a charter to Telegraph Creek down in B.C., and Herman Peterson from Atlin was completing our work into Fairweather Lake. We had two other aircraft ourselves, but they were not equipped to operate off the river, and there was no flight strip at Ole Wickstrom's wood camp.

My normal route to base from Minto would have been straight south on the

Yukon to Carmacks; up the Nordenskiold Valley past Twin Lakes to Braeburn Lake; between Fox Lake and Lake Laberge, and so to Whitehorse.

The camp was on the stretch of the Yukon River that flows westerly towards Carmacks and was situated between the Little Salmon and Big Salmon Rivers, on the north bank. Coming south from Minto, then, I swung to the east at Five Finger Rapids, flew up Tatchum Creek to Tatchum Lake, by Frenchman Lake, down a little piece of the Little Salmon River, and so to the Yukon.

At the camp the deep water was below a gravel bank, so we tied the Sea-Bee up at this point, and the Indians brought down the sick woman on a stretcher. We sent back for a saw to cut the handles from the stretcher so it would fit into the aircraft with one front seat taken out, and in this way we managed to get her aboard. Another woman was to ride with her and carry her baby—a tiny bundle neatly wrapped up and pinned, with even its face covered with the wrappings.

When all was ready, the people on the shore went back and disappeared without further ado, so I started the motor, ran it up and backed out. The woman on the stretcher was a fairly husky looking girl, but her face was deathly pale. She really looked ill, and moaned sometimes in her breathing. Her companion was crying softly to herself.

By now it was a pleasant sunny afternoon, and as there was little or no wind I turned to take off downstream because this would add from six to eight miles an hour to my speed through the air and assist with the take off.

The propeller came out of reverse when I moved the control forwards, but the blades would not move into a position that would give me a forward motion. I shut the engine off and, looking back upstream to the place we had left for some help, saw there was nobody there. We were making good time downstream in the current, and were now beyond the point where I could shout and expect to be heard.

We had swung around and were drifting backward and, looking back through the open door, I could see where the wing tip would come close to the bank with any luck. Accordingly, with a tie rope, I climbed out up onto the wing, tied the rope to the lifting lug, and as the distance between the wing tip and the river bank narrowed moved out and jumped and was able to pull the aircraft in and tie it to the exposed root of a tree on the river bank.

It was with considerable relief that I made the shore with one end of a line that was securely tied at the other end to my aircraft. At least now we were not certainly subject to the vagaries of wind and current, but we were not out of the woods either by any manner of means.

I assured the passengers that something required fixing, and we should be getting away shortly. Luckily the unfortunate souls were much too pre-occupied with their own difficulties to be acutely aware of what was happening. They did not appear to be alarmed in any way.

It was discovered that two small screws had worked loose and then sheared off, but that I could still fasten the blades in firmly in forward fine pitch. The propeller would not now be adjustable, but it would work as a fixed pitch. It was opportune that it had to be in fine pitch, because we would not have been able to take off the water with the propeller fixed in a coarse pitch.

With the propeller rigged to the extent that it would at least get us home, we started up. I pushed the nose out into the stream and climbed in again.

A straight course to Whitehorse would take us along Claire Lake and so to the north end of Lake Laberge and on south to base. Flying time would be roughly fifty minutes.

We took off, and it was then I became aware of the fact that I was in for more trouble—possible trouble, that is—but at least I was aware of it.

The propeller was now fixed in fine pitch and we could cruise in fine pitch with higher RPM than normal with no ill effects other than a very high fuel consumption. The difficulty would be that with high RPM the speeded-up oil pump would be forcing crankcase oil through the plugged or restricted oil cooler at an indicated high oil pressure that tells me something has got to give, and when it gives I know that we must come down.

The oil pressure can be reduced by reducing the engine speed, but this in turn reduces the flying speed. We must, in the circumstances, go on. There was no point in going back anywhere. We must not only go on, but we must arrive at Whitehorse, and every effort must be made to keep the aircraft flying. I was appalled at the thought of being forced down somewhere on the river with a passenger so deathly ill, and no possible aid in sight until late the following day.

There have been other tight situations I remember, that have provided me with plenty of food for thought at the time. Situations that had the worst come to the worst, would have been awkward in the extreme.

I recall, for instance, being sent to Carmacks on one occasion to pick up a young Indian woman who had already been in labour for three days. The doctor had been requested to come down river to attend to her, but had preferred to have her brought in instead. I was provided with a hypo of morphine, was told to "give her this and fetch her in". As it happened, everything turned out fine. She had a breach presentation and seemingly could not have had the child without the doctor's help. At the time, of course, I was not aware of this, and all the way home with her I was wondering how to have a baby with one hand and fly with the other.

On that occasion there had been no real peril, and the discussion of the situation thereafter provided us with considerable amusement.

I had a feeling that today was different.

There was no alternative but a compromise to be made between a safe flying speed and a relatively safe oil pressure for the restricted oil cooler, so I throttled back the engine immediately. The pressure was certainly higher than it should be, so I dared not risk the overland route that would shorten our flying time considerably. As well, it would require an increase in engine speed to climb to any height and I did not wish to risk this either, especially when it was not entirely necessary.

We could fly low, but in doing that we must stay over the water so as to sit down with safety if we had to. So we stayed over the river at a couple of hundred feet, for every twist and turn that it makes. If I had dared to risk a climb to some two or three thousand feet we could have flown in a straight line, keeping the river always within gliding distance.

We flew up past Big Salmon, south to Hootalinqua, along the Thirty Mile to Laberge, up Laberge and then into the Lewis (now the Yukon) and so to Whitehorse.

By the time we were ten miles out from the aerodrome I was able to get control tower on the radio so that they knew we were coming and where we were, and it was okay then to risk a climb. We needed to gain enough height for a glide to the river should something happen while crossing the dry land between the river and the aerodrome. At this time the tower was requested to have an ambulance there when we landed.

It had taken us almost two hours to travel a distance that would normally have taken about fifty minutes as the crow flies. While the aircraft's speed was slower than normal, the engine speed was higher than normal, and this of course increased our fuel consumption.

At the control tower the Army ambulance was waiting, and it was there that the three passengers were discharged. When I started up again to taxi along the strip to our hanger, the engine stopped by itself. We were out of gas!

I was sorry to learn that the young mother died that night in hospital, and have many times wondered where the tiny baby is now. He or she would be thirty years old. The fateful trip for its mother was in 1948.

Yukon Yarns

Yukon Yarns

1921: A group of Yukoners photographed before heading "outside" for a holiday to Edmonton. Most had recently returned by dog team from staking oil claims at Norman Wells (a 22-day trip). Back row, left to right: Victor Bullock, McDonald, John Olson, Tucker (Agent), Houle MacKenzie, Tom Bee. Front row: Joe Ladue, Guder, Pat Pelly, Frank Etzel.

Tom Tracy

When he landed in Canada from County Mayo in Ireland, Tom Tracy headed for Mayo in the Yukon Territory, and that is where he spent his days, mostly. He was well known and well thought of in Dawson as well, and very occassionally he came down to Whitehorse. It would be more correct to say that Tracy came up to Whitehorse, rather than down, because travel was always by river and it is here that the rivers flow "down" north. It's hard to get used to the idea, when north is universally at the top of the map.

Tom was fairly tall and handsome, with an engaging and likeable personality—a rather typical carefree Irishman. When I knew him we worked together in a labour gang at the Whitehorse Airport in 1949. He and I were the only two that were actually doing much work. The rest of them, it is supposed, were typical of labour gangs anywhere.

Like most of the Mayo old timers, Tom had some "ground" as they say; that is a mining claim, on which he built a cabin. Whenever he was able to get a few bucks ahead he was able to spend some time developing his property; and the story goes that he invited a geologist out to have a look at his claim.

The man was indifferently impressed with Tom's ground it seemed, for he kicked a few rocks around, looked at the lay of the land, and said, "No, you've got nothin' here Tracy."

"Well, anyway, come down to the cabin", says Tracy, "and we'll have a couple of hot rums before you go back."

So, down they went to Tracy's cabin for a drink; and when they got inside the man noticed that Tracy's stove was on blocks about four feet off the floor, and he sat fascinated as Tracy lit the stove and reached up to put the kettle on top.

Soon they had had a couple of hot O.P.'s (overproof rum), and it was not until then that the geologist asked Tracy why he had his stove so high in the air.

"Mother of God!" says Tracy, "you come up on me claim and look down through fifteen feet of solid rock and you can see that there is nothin' there. Now you come down into me cabin and you can't see that I haven't got enough of stove pipe to put me stove on the floor!"

George Bacon

George Bacon was a north country Englishman, judging by his accent, but he had been in Canada most of his life. He too, like most of the old timers around Mayo, had some good ground; which he subsequently sold to the company, built a nice home in Victoria, B.C. and moved his family there. He had also spent a lot of time around Tulsequa in northern B.C. on the Taku Inlet, and he came back every summer and worked for the Government at keeping the streams clear of logs and log jams.

It was my job on the Hydrometric Survey during those days to measure the volume of water in the Taku River and its tributaries, and our party always stayed with George Bacon on those occasions. We were not expected to bring grub with us, but he was never averse to the arrival of a case or so of beer. And so it was that we spent a few pleasant evenings yarning after a day's work on the waterways. One evening we got on the subject of false teeth, so he started to tell us of his two old friends in Mayo some years back.

The older man of the two kept complaining to the doctor of headaches, dizzy spells and spots in front of his eyes. These two old fellows had some good ground they had been working on for years and, of course, they lived on the property. On one of their trips to town, the doctor recommended the removal of the old fellow's teeth as a remedy for his trouble.

A month or so later, because he was still plagued with his headaches, etc., they removed his appendix; and then subsequently his gall bladder.

Luckily for the old fellow, about this time they sold their claims to the company for $100,000.00, which gave them $50,000.00 each, so they decided to take a trip to Vancouver. They had not left the north or been "outside" for 30 years, and they also figured to have the old man's difficulty looked into by an expert medical authority before he ran out of parts.

Accordingly they made the trip to Whitehorse by paddle wheeler; to Skagway by narrow gauge railroad; and then to Vancouver by coastal steamer. They arrived in Vancouver still in their bib overalls.

Right away they agreed they should get some new clothes, city clothes, and so they went to a men's store and got fitted out. When they were out in the street again, the younger man said to the old fellow, "you didn't get a new hat!"

"Nothing wrong with this hat", says the old fellow, "I've had it for years. It's a damn good hat!"

"Well, I'm not walking down the street with you unless you get a new hat to match the rest of your new outfit."

So back they went to the store, and the old fellow said to the clerk, "I guess I'll have to buy a new hat."

"Yes sir, what size do you take?"

"6 & ⅞."

"Yes sir, I'll measure your head if you like, and we can tell exactly."

"6 & ⅞ is my size!"

"According to the measure you should wear size 7 & ⅛."

"Look here young fellow, I've been wearing 6 & ⅞ for years and years, that's my size, and that's the size I want."

"Yes sir, but if you wear a size that is too small you are likely to have headaches, dizzy spells and spots in front of your eyes."

Tom Meekins

Tom Meekins is a typical cowpoke type of man; tall, thin, taciturn. In the summer he always wears western work clothes, big belt buckle, riding boots, stetson hat, the sleeves of his shirt buttoned at the wrist, and arm bands like fancy women's garters. He works as a horse wrangler in the big game guide and outfitter industry during the late summer and fall, and in the winter he is a trapper and a good one too.

He was one of four or five of us sitting around Danny Nowlan's front room at Danny's game farm near Takhini Hot Springs. It was Sunday afternoon and Danny's wife, Erika, kept filling the tea pot and we all kept drinking the tea, as was our habit. We were talking about the two wolves Danny had, and of how one of them had bitten the end off one of his father-in-law's fingers, and the talk was generally about wolves.

Meekins was rolling a cigarette, and when he got it licked and neatly finished he twisted one end and then sat regarding his effort quizzically. There was a lull in the conversation, and it could be seen that he was getting ready to say something. For my part I thought he was going to say something about the cigarette.

"Wolves are the darndest critters I ever encountered. It is uncanny how clever they are, how they work together in pairs, each one seeming to know what is required of him. They even seem to be able to tell what a man is thinking and what he is going to do next.

He had established his control of the conversation, engaged our interest and so we sat still while he continued.

"Several years ago I was in the McQuestion country, trapping. I was three days out. Three days steady snow shoeing before I reached my cabin, when I became aware of the fact that I was being followed; there were two big wolves back on the trail, a big gray, and an even bigger black one. During the daytime they kept well back out of rifle range; they seemed to know about men and guns but they were always there.

At night they came in close and circled my camp; and I built up a bigger fire, and sometimes I could see a pair of eyes watching me and shining in the reflected fire light. When they saw me watching them or making a move for my gun, the light would go out as they turned and moved farther back. It gives a man an eerie feeling to be miles out and away from everything and know that two big predators have been following the trail and were even now circling the camp.

"This was hungry country, no game at all, and I was surprised that they should even be there in the circumstances. On top of this I had no dog with me and I left no scraps for them to clean up; and so, given time for sober reflection, there was only one conclusion that I could arrive at—that they had me trussed and dressed for their next meal.

"There seemed to be something peculiar about this, because normally a man in the woods armed with a good rifle is the lord of all he surveys, and doesn't have to be apprehensive of anything. Wolves, and even grizzly bears, keep out of his way if they happen to see him first. But these two wolves had seen me first, they were on my trail, they were out there right now, and they seemed to have followed me with a singleness of purpose that made me feel uneasy. Now why should I feel uneasy? I have spent most of my life in the woods in the north here, and I know, also, that wolves do not attack a man when he is on his feet; but just let them catch me down or asleep with the camp fire burned out, and a man just might have something to worry about."

We all knew what he said was true. There has never been a real authenticated instance of a man being attacked by a wolf or even wolves; but there was a good possibility of it if a man was obviously at a disadvantage and the wolves were hungry enough.

"Naturally, I had my rifle", Meekins continued, "but I only had two rounds of ammunition left. Of course those two wolves did not know this, but from the way they behaved you would think they did and that they were anxious for me to expend those two rounds, and then I was a goner. When the fire was good I slept fitfully until it went low, and then I would wake up in a hurry and pile her up again. I was getting to the point where I needed sleep.

"In the morning I could see where they had circled my camp, where they had sat and watched, probably licking their chops, the bastards! They had come in very close in the darkness, but with the daylight they moved back, but I didn't see them at all until I stopped on a rise to have a smoke and take a rest, and sure enough there they were way back on the trail, the big black actually sitting down looking my way, while the gray was moving about.

"I figured I would have to try to get them that night some way or other, because I simply must sleep; and so late, when I stopped and it got dark, I sat all night with my back against a tree, two fires—one to the right and one to the left—because I wanted to be able to see through between them. I kept my rifle cradled in my left arm and my right hand where it should be. I had only to slide it out of its mit and my finger was on the trigger. I kept awake. Several times I saw their eyes shining, but when I raised the rifle the lights went out. The crafty sons-o-bitches! I was going to have to resort to some sort of guile or one-upmanship if I wanted to get back, and I had one more night and two days to get through. I wondered if I could manage to stay awake.

"Luckily, the next day there was a place that could be reached before dark where a fellow could camp with his back against a bluff and only have a half circle out in front to worry about. When I got there at the end of the day I got in a pile of fire wood, cut two bushy jack pines and lay them in front of me between the fire and the wall, and there is where I sat. I figured the wolves might get curious enough to come in, and they would not be able to see me when I raised the gun.

"I was some sleepy, but I had to sit fairly still and this made it even harder to stay awake. Several times I caught my head nodding but from sheer desperation, born of the desire to stay alive and get back, I stayed alert long enough to see that first pair of eyes directly out in front and close in. I could scarcely suppress a smile as I carefully raised my gun and put a bullet between those two blasted shining orbs. Out they went—bingo!

"I figured the other one would take off in a hurry, but no—must have been his mate that I killed. There were his two eyes off to the side a piece. Without waiting a second I put my last bullet between them, and out they went. Then, hardly moving, I settled back to go to sleep at last."

"I couldn't believe it", Meekins was saying, "when I saw those eyes again across the camp fire. Not one pair, but two, just the same as before. I couldn't believe it.

"Do you know what those god damn wolves had done?"

He looked around with a dumbfounded expression on his face.

"They sat side by side, the bastards, each with his outside eye closed, and I fired my last two bullets between them!"

Firth River
Gold Rush

Harry Gordon-Cooper

Firth River
Gold Rush

The Million-Dollar Ditch bringing water to Dawson.

Gold—to be had for the taking—riches overnight—adventure—excitement —all spelled out in the magic words "gold rush—stampede".

Pool Field had discovered rich placer ground in the Firth River Valley in the Canadian Arctic, and when the word came out the rush was on.

The Firth River empties into the Arctic Ocean south of Herschel Island on a bleak, barren, windy coast that is considered to be the most inhospitable area in the whole Arctic, especially in the spring, with the season of 40-mile-an-hour winds that inhibit travel by even the best of man and dogs.

The valley itself, of course, lies back from the coast, and the river finds the sea after travelling through a deep canyon which, because of the winds, is known as the "Blow Hole".

Word of the stampede soon reached Whitehorse, and a group of businessmen immediately decided to send in stakers and acquire some placer claims along the Firth River. A placer claim is 1500 feet along a stream, and each person can stake one claim for himself and two more by proxy for other persons.

And so it was that Curly Desrosiers, Alex Van Bibber and myself headed north from Whitehorse to the Firth Valley to stake nine claims along the river, the expedition being financed by the six men who wanted claims by proxy.

It was March, 1948, still very much winter in these latitudes, and for an aeroplane we took a three-seater Piper Super Cruiser equipped with an aeromatic propeller and skis. Our route should have been north to Dawson, then north again from Dawson 300 miles to Old Crow and then north again into the Firth Valley. This was the best route, but it was not possible because we could not refuel at Old Crow; so it was decided to go via Fort MacPherson and Aklavik where aviation gas was available, then northwest to Herschel Island.

Initially we planned to land at Herschel Island, engage the services of Eskimos and dogs, journey into the valley, stake our ground, return to Herschel and fly home from there—a good plan which never came to pass.

For three men for such a trip there was required a fair amount of gear and grub, and when we had it assembled it took an imposing amount of space and respresented a considerable weight for our aircraft to carry.

The mandatory emergency gear for aircraft flying commercially in these latitudes consisted of one sleeping bag per person, one axe, one rifle and ammunition, a first aid kit, nose tent, and blow pot for warming up the aeroplane engine, one pair of snowshoes, extra oil, funnel and chamois for refueling, pocket compass and maps, matches and dry rations.

In addition to this of course, we carried a tent with a stovepipe safety, a Teslin stove, snowshoes for Curly (Alex was to pick up his in Dawson), our personal packs containing extra clothing, moccasins, socks, camera, towel, razor and tooth brushes, etc.

Warming up the engine at Fort MacPherson.

Our grub was kept to a minimum, as there was no point in carrying food to places along the route where we could always purchase what we required. There were the dry rations for emergency.

The Super Cruiser has one seat in the front for the pilot, one wide seat for two persons back of that, and a small luggage space behind that again. A plywood bulkhead separates this area from the fuselage, and this we removed in order to sling the light, bulky sleeping bags and snowshoes from the center longeron down inside the fuselage.

Finally everything was stowed, still with room for ourselves. We climbed in, started up and headed for Dawson. Our speed would be from 90 to 100 miles per hour, our route over a distance of some 350 miles. Fuel tanks would keep us aloft for five hours, so we were in good shape for the first leg of the journey.

Apart from the Alaska Highway, which traversed the southern part of the Territory, and a road south from Whitehorse to Carcross and Tagish, there were no roads in the Yukon in those days. All the traffic north of Whitehorse was by river boat during the summer, and by air, when necessary, during winter.

Heading north, we flew between Fox Lake and Lake Laberge, ("...that night on the marge of Lake Laberge I cremated Sam McGee..." from the famous pen of Robert Service) On past Braeburn Lake, Twin Lakes, and subsequently into the Nordenskjold Valley and on over to Carmacks.

Carmacks is situated 100 miles north of Whitehorse, at a point where the Yukon River changes its course from westerly to northerly. It was a small community consisting of a Taylor and Drury store and trading post, a telegraph office, a roadhouse for the winter stage route to Dawson that no longer operated , the cabins of a few trappers, miners, and prospectors, and an Indian village. It bore the name of George Carmack, the co-discoverer of gold on the Klondike River in 1896.

From Carmacks we continued north to Minto, a river boat wood camp on the Yukon River, and there turned easterly and made for Pelly Crossing on the Pelly River. This was Alex Van Bibber's home, and as we passed over he pointed out the hill with one grave on it, and the river flat below with the large old log house and other buildings. His father, Ira Van Bibber, a West Virginian "Ridge Runner", and his Indian wife had settled there forty odd years ago, and had raised a fine family with only a good garden, traps and a rifle.

From Pelly Crossing, we travelled still easterly to Hungry Mountain on the Stewart River. The Stewart follows a course almost parallel to the Pelly on its way to join the Yukon. Off to the south and east some twenty odd miles is the town of Mayo, and a little north of Mayo are the rich silver mines known a Keno Hill, Calumet, and Elsa.

At Stewart Crossing we turned north again, crossed the McQuestion, flew along the Flat River Valley to the fabulous Klondike River, and so to Dawson. We landed on the river in front of the town, and spent the evening with Alex's folks who were in Dawson for the winter.

This was an interesting evening indeed. While Curly and myself talked with Mr. Van Bibber, we were able to watch Alex and his mother fill the center portion of a pair of snowshoes with heavy rawhide lacing. The top and bottom portions had already been filled with fine, light babeesh, so that when the centers were filled the snowshoes were ready to go. We each, now, had a pair.

This was the first time I had met Ira Van Bibber, and Curly and myself discovered that he must take his place in the realm of fabulous story tellers. As we watched the snowshoe filling process, we learned how, as a young man, he and his brother had packed supplies over the White Pass during the gold rush for a man subsequently known throughout the north as "Whiskey Sullivan". He told us of the snow slide that claimed so many lives, and of the almost unbelievable stories that are connected with it.

He told us of how he had met "Shorty" (Mrs. Van Bibber); of how he trapped and hunted, and raised his family. It was at this time that I decided to put these fabulous yarns into print, and over the years of our acquaintance have been able in a measure to do this. Nothing could equal his gift for narrative. No writer, however skilled, could ever capture for the enjoyment of his reader, the same delight experienced by Ira Van Bibber's listeners.

The following day, before we proceeded further, it was felt we should make some slight adjustment to the aeromatic propeller on the aircraft, because we were carrying much more of a load than was normal.

The aeromatic propeller is one that, by means of fly weights, adjusts its own pitch according to the speed it is travelling through the air and the amount of thrust it is receiving from the engine. This type of propeller, as can be seen, provides more efficient power for take off, and then adjusts itself for economical cruising. It's an idea that is very efficient, but its operation requires a slight modification of the take-off technique.

It needed, at this time, to be set up a little, and this we did by the addition of washers to the fly weights. After flight testing it twice, we spent the remainder of the day making the acquaintance of Dawson and its people.

The city itself sits on swampy ground, underneath which is perma frost. It is considered that millions of dollars in gold still lies frozen in the muck way beneath the surface. One day they may turn the area of the townsite upside down, as had been done to the broad Klondike Valley, recover the gold, and rebuild the town on the tailings.

It would improve the drainage of the area and preclude the business of having the buildings heave in such a crazy fashion as they do because of the freezing and thawing of the poorly drained ground on which the town sits.

We stayed at the hotel, and could not help but be amused by the slant and twist of the hallways and the rooms. In the lobby downstairs were the three famous nudes from the Old Flora Dora Saloon. Oil paintings that stretch almost from floor to ceiling. Some years later these three famous pictures were put up for sale for $1,000.00 When it transpired nobody seemed to have that kind of money to be used for that purpose, they were given to the Dawson museum and were lost when the museum burned.

We met Vic Foley, the former Canadian boxing champion and many of the old timers who had been there since the gold rush days. We then planned our flight for the morning.

We had an opportunity to meet and talk with Pat Callison, who operated his own bush outfit based at Dawson. Pat had returned recently from the Firth River, and showed us where he had flown right into the valley and landed on a bench by the river; so we decided to do this also. It would certainly save us a considerable amount of both time and expense.

Accordingly we took off the following morning. It was a beautiful day. Clear sky and not much wind. The distance to Fort MacPherson was calculated to be some 450 to 500 miles. We had, we figured, some five hours flying to do, and we had five hours fuel in our tanks. We took on the additional weight of a ten-gallon drum of gas to be on the safe side.

Our route, this time, took us northerly and easterly, up and over the Seela Pass and thence down the Blackstone River to either the Hart River, which joins the Peel, or to the headwaters of the Peel itself; and then past the mouths of the Wind, Bonnet Plume and Snake, and so on down north on the Peel to Fort MacPherson.

The map, in those days, showed nothing for 100 miles on the far side of the Seela Pass but a dotted line which indicated what was thought to be the location of the Blackstone River; but as we were flying into the apex of a triangle formed by the Peel and the Hart Rivers we were bound to come upon either one or the other, so we felt safe enough.

Tombstone Mountain, a massive, black, slabsided mountain that stands out amongst its snow covered fellows, was on our right as we flew along; and we had been able previously to see the "million dollar ditch" that brought extra water to the gold operations at the turn of the century. It had cost one million dollars to build. It had enabled large scale hydraulic gold dredging viable for another 50 years.

Soon we were through the Pass and headed down the other side. It was a fine, clear day, and we held our height in order to be able to see farther, and then eventually down a long valley to our right we were able to see the white path of what we decided was the Hart River.

We knew we must find our way back over virtually the same route in order to get into the Pass from the north east side, so before turning to head for the Hart we circled and photographed the mountains and land marks at the point of turning.

It had not occurred to us that we would not be able to get the pictures processed until after we had arrived back; but the very act of circling and photographing had the effect of impressing the area on our memories; and we had no difficulty in recognizing the place again.

Somewhere off to the right was Hungry Lake, where Pat Callison had landed on his return from the Arctic a few days ago. Here he found a trapper on the verge of starvation, and brought him back to Dawson. It would appear that Hungry Lake and the area surrounding it are well named.

We followed the Hart River along deep canyons, and eventually to where it joins the Peel. Now we were over mapped country again, and every bend in the river below could be followed on the map.

Nearing Fort MacPherson, the Yukon-Northwest Territories border, as indicated on the map, appeared below. It cannot be seen except from almost directly above, but there it was; slashed out and running east and west as straight as a die away from both sides of the river.

Generally the landing strip on the river at a small settlement is well marked with small evergreens stuck into the snow; but for some reason or other, at Fort MacPherson, we missed the well packed strip and landed in the deep crusted snow in the wrong place, and sank as we slowed down. We were soon, however, surrounded by Indians from the river bank who came down with teams of dogs and toboggans. They pulled us out onto the hard surface, where we could taxi again, and from where we could proceed to the proper place.

The flight time from Dawson was 4 hours and 45 minutes.

We put on the nose tent, drained the oil, tied down the wings, and put the skis on sticks to keep them clear of the snow. Had we not done this, the skis would have been frozen tight to the snow in the morning.

A nose tent is a covering for the engine. It has a sleeve into which goes one blade of the propeller. It hangs to the ground all around, and ties across underneath. In the morning we would light the blow pot, put it in the tent under the motor, put the oil on top of it, and heat both the engine and the oil at the same time.

We were invited to dinner, and to stay the night, by the Hudson Bay factor and his wife. This was appreciated because it spared us the necessity of breaking out our tent, sleeping bags, and other gear which was tightly stowed in the plane.

The factor was an Englishman, and both he and his Canadian wife were in love with the Arctic and preferred living there to anywhere else. They would, they said, much rather live on the coast and not up the river in the mud, as he called it. Previously they had been stationed at Tuktoyaktuk; and his wife told of how she had enjoyed getting out on the hard, crusted snow with her dogs and sleigh. She explained that on the open Arctic the dogs are hitched so that they spread out like a fan, and that they are directed by sending the whip out on the snow on the opposite side of the turn desired. In the wooded country around Fort MacPherson the Loucheux Indians hook the dogs up single file to facilitate following the trails in the bush and along the river.

They provided us with a pleasant and interesting visit. In the morning we purchased a small primus stove and a can of coal oil. We got away late, but this did not matter as we only had to fly to Aklavik, some fifty miles further down the river. We poured into the fuel tanks the ten gallons of gas in the drum we carried with us, got the engine and the oil warmed up and, after taking some pictures of colourfully dressed girls, took off once more.

We flew over a maze of islands, oxbow lakes and channels such as cannot be seen except in the Mackenzie Delta. We flew until we had Black Mountain on our left beam, and did not see Aklavik until it was directly below us.

Here it was that the first signs of gold rush became evident. Along the river bank were mining and exploration company aircraft, together with an assortment of smaller ski-equipped aircraft flown in by other adventurous individuals like ourselves.

I had pictured Aklavik as a small cluster of log buildings on the bank of the river with the Union Jack flying above the Mounted Police post. Here was a village with streets, electric light poles, a modern Hudson Bay store, essentially the same as any small community to be found outside.

There were some differences, however, we soon discovered; we were unable to purchase any three inch stove pipe for our Teslin stove. Most of the people of Aklavik had recently installed chemical toilets in their houses, and as a result of this there had been a run on three inch stove pipe.

There was a sleigh dog tied to every fence post, tree or electric pole that could be seen. Spring was in the offing and the muskrat season on the Mackenzie Delta was about to begin. Trappers and their families were gathering ahead of time for the opening of the short season, and Aklavik was the focal point.

Most of these people were in an affluent state—Eskimo for most part—but there was a smattering of Norwegians, Swedes and others, all with native wives and colourfully attired families.

It was considered expedient to spend a few days in Aklavik to enjoy and participate in the general atmosphere of excitement, plus the fact that we wanted to get as much information as we could before proceeding into the valley.

The author, Alex VanBibber, and Curly Desrosiers at the Aklavik radio station.

We had brought with us a couple of bottles of overproof rum, and had no difficulty in making the acquaintance of many knowing persons from whom we were able to get information. We had to be careful, nevertheless, to conserve our rum for the purpose for which we had brought it. There is nothing in the world that so effectively prepares a man to consider the world through rose-coloured glasses than a steaming mug of hot rum while supper is being prepared. Generally the first thing that is attended to when making camp is a billy of hot water for the hot rum. When the word got around that we had a bottle, it had to be quickly established that there was only one.

In the Territories, and anywhere else in Canada for that matter, it is not permitted by law to traffic commercially in any way with wild meat such as moose, caribou, etc. There was no commercial beef, pork, or mutton left in town, so we ate bacon and eggs for breakfast and lunch at the hotel and were able to get for $1 a good big helping of stewed rabbit at the establishment of a former Mounted Police officer named Bell; and this, with plentiful bread, butter and potatoes, we enjoyed for supper.

Mr. Bell was, in our eyes, a very enterprising gentleman. He had a big roomy place with a juke box, and apart from the stewed snowshoe rabbit he did a flourishing business selling ice cream at the counter and ice for water at twenty-five cents a block to the Eskimos. It seemed a little incongruous to us that the Eskimos should be buying ice from a white man in the Arctic, but nevertheless there it was.

There is a radio station with Eskimo announcers and personnel, which broadcasts Eskimo songs and dances, and provides a service of broadcast personal messages and news to outlying areas. Everybody is kept in touch with what is going on.

Sometimes there was a show to be seen in one of the buildings, but mostly we gathered with the other participants in the gold rush, and soon formed our opinions of most of them as stampeders. We had the feeling sometimes that there was more gold being mined in the hotel lobby than would ever be taken from the Firth River Valley.

Before long we loaded up again and took off. Our route this time took us north to the Arctic Ocean, west along the coast to Herschel Island, then south up the Firth River from the coast and so into the Firth River Valley.

We had gas in our tanks and a ten gallon drum for six and a half hours flying, and considered this would take us in and back out again with some to spare. It was roughly 200 miles in and 200 miles out, a total of about five hours flying which could be affected one way or another according to the vagaries of wind and weather.

Eventually we arrived over the coast and swung westerly toward Herschel Island. Here the variation or the difference between magnetic north on Boothia

The MacKenzie Delta.

Peninsula, in the Canadian Arctic which is where the aircraft compass needle points, and the actual north pole, which is roughly fifteen hundred north of it, is, in the area in which we were flying, some forty degrees easterly. We knew then that the direction of the actual north pole was forty degrees less than "the north" our compass needle indicated.

When we directed our gaze in this direction we saw nothing as far as the horizon but white Arctic ice and snow. We were looking out over the Beaufort Sea and there was no land whatsoever between ourselves and the north pole— an interesting thing to contemplate.

On this part of the coast we encountered a strong southwest wind, and turned our aircraft into it in order to make good a track over the ground. This had the effect of reducing our ground speed. The geographical features of the coast are well defined on the map nevertheless, so it was a simple matter to time our flight between Shingle Point and Kay Point to determine that the speed at which travelled over the surface was sixty miles per hour. The air speed indicator showed we were moving through the air at ninety-five miles an hour. The difference amounted to a loss of thirty-five miles an hour.

We had been in the air for one and a half hours at Kay Point, and the loss of ground speed would affect us for a measure of time inside a further one and a half hours, so we knew we had no cause for concern.

It is interesting to note that an aircraft flying a given distance into a wind that reduces its speed through the air, does not gain this loss back by turning and flying the same track back in the opposite direction. The reason for this is that the aircraft is under the influence of the adverse wind for a longer period of time.

We had been looking forward to landing at Herschel Island, even though we had intended to fly into the Firth Valley. The reason for our intended stop over was that the Royal Canadian Mounted Police Vessel, St. Roche, was frozen in at Herschel on her historic east-to-west transit of the fabled Northwest Passage, and her second and last circumnavigation of the North American continent.

We decided, nevertheless, that it was such a fine day aloft and we could see what we considered to be the mouth of the Firth, and coupled with the fact that Herschel Island itself was mostly obscured in a mist, that we should fly on in and accomplish what we had come to do, and then visit the St. Roche on the way home.

We swung, therefore, towards the break in the hills where the river comes out onto the coast, and followed its course south. We knew for certain that this was the river we were looking for when we spotted the horseshoe bend clearly indicated on the map. Soon we saw two other aircraft on the bench that had been marked for us by Pat Callison, and set our aircraft down on hard, crusted snow.

With us we had brought a bundle of sticks to be used in preparing the aircraft for an extended stay. Since we had no idea of the availability of such material at the place we figured to land, we brought them with us. There was, as it happened, a smattering of trees about, but having brought these sticks with us certainly spared us the necessity of having to rustle new ones.

Two were put under each ski to keep the skis up off the hard crusted snow, and one went under the tail ski. The snow was crusted to a depth of about four inches, and when a hole was cut in this under each wing tie the last remaining sticks, with tie ropes made fast to the middle, were placed under the crust like a toggle and the loose snow packed on top again. The packed snow soon freezes solid like the crust, and the aircraft sits securely bound to the ground.

We tied her down first thing because of the wind. That done, the nose tent went on and the oil was drained.

By this time we had visitors. They had a camp a mile away in the shelter of some bush, and they helped us pack our tent and supplies to the same location.

We soon had a small clearing in the bush and our tent in place. Both Alex and Curly are men reared in the north and are familiar with life in the bush, so we were able to cope remarkably well. When it was discovered we had no stove pipe for our Teslin stove, we were invited to do our cooking in the other tent, and this offer we were grateful to accept.

Because of the weight factor, we carried very little of our food in cans, but we had plenty of bacon and eggs, flour, dehydrated potatoes, bread, butter, jam, sugar, tea, raisins and chocolate. It was hoped that we could secure some wild meat, but the Firth is hungry country and during our sojourn there we did not see so much as a ptarmigan.

Discovery claim was about five miles up river from the camp, but we had learned in Aklavik that the river was staked solid for twenty miles as far as

Sheep Creek, and up Sheep Creek for another six miles. We realized we must go way up the river to get any ground at all, so accordingly we made up our packs and set forth the following day without further ado.

Most of the river runs in a deep canyon, and we descended to the bottom of this and followed the river. The geology of the area as indicated on the walls of the canyon shows thin stratas that are heaved, curled and bent to a remarkable degree and in many places give the appearance that the whole area is standing on edge.

From the point of view of placer mining, this fact is interesting because the river bed, being composed of tilted stratas of some soft and some hard layers, naturally became grooved, sometimes at right angles to the flow of water thus providing natural riffles for any gold to settle in. We were told that at low water in the spring, if a loose piece of strata could be found and lifted out, that the gold in the bottom could be scooped out with a spoon. This may sound ridiculous, but it is in fact entirely conceivable.

From the time we set out we travelled steadily for the remainder of the day and on into the night, which did not get very dark and then only for a short while. At 3:00 a.m. it was growing lighter and we figured we were near the mouth of Sheep Creek. By this time we were weary and our shoulders were sore from the packs. Sheep Creek or no, there seemed to be nothing in the world more important than a rest.

The snow on the river was crusted but not strong enough to hold a man up without snowshoes, so we were compelled to keep them on during the whole distance. Snowshoeing on a hard surface, as we did that day, was pleasant because the shoes on such a hard surface provide a little spring to each step, which is helpful. We had, however, been travelling for too long a period continuously, and by now a rest was indicated.

Accordingly we dropped our packs. Alex thought he would like to take a look around the next bend, so he left his pack with us and took off. Curly and I climbed the bank, and while I lit a fire he made a windbreak of small trees piled behind us. We made some tea and ate raisins and nuts, and felt considerably refreshed.

In about an hour Alex returned. He had found the camp of John McGinnes and Anchor Hoydle. He had some tea and a rest, then three of us made our way straight to our friends' camp where we were made welcome, the way of the north.

These men had been in the valley for a month, and were really the only men of the many taking part in the stampede who were not mining in the hotel in Aklavik. At the mouth of the Sheep Creek they had sunk a shaft to bed rock to test the values of the gravel there. This had entailed cutting and hauling wood with the dog team, because it was necessary to build fires and thaw the ground as they went. They had whip-sawed lumber from the small trees to make a square pail for hauling up the muck as the shaft got deeper. They had no fresh meat. They still had plenty of grub, but both they and the dogs were thin from hard work.

At our first camp at the bottom end of the valley we had cut boughs to sleep on, but here we were given dried caribou skins for an underlay; and there is nothing finer for an insulation against the cold that comes from underneath than caribou hair which is hollow and has the ability to trap more air.

We discovered from our friends that Sheep Creek was staked for a distance of eight miles. We rested a day and a night, then slipped into the squaw hitch of our snowshoes and headed up Sheep Creek to get nine claims on what appeared to be the last open ground on the creek or the river.

We carried nothing with us but some lunch, an axe and a gun. This was a relief, because the muscles across our shoulders and necks were sore to the extent that even the strap from my camera gave me discomfort.

During the morning on the way up it was sunny and warm. The snow was thawing and our moccasins became wet. As the day wore on and we ascended higher, the air grew colder and it was more pleasant travelling.

Every 1,500 feet was a stake of some description, and when we reached the last one we added nine more, which took us to the fork at the top. A legal stake is required to be four feet high with the top 18 inches squared into four inch surfaces. There was certainly no tree in the neighbourhood that could boast of these proportions, so we used the small scrubby trees, a few of which were along the river. Though they were a couple of inches through, when cut off at four feet with the branches trimmed and one side smoothed off with an axe to provide a surface to write on, they made do.

On the way down it was colder. Our moccasins froze and rubbed the skin on our feet a little where the snowshoe ties had cut in when the moosehide was wet. We also had difficulty and some discomfort from balls of ice that formed on the rawhide of the snowshoes beneath the transverse arch of our feet. It became necessary to carry a stick or use the axe handle to keep breaking the ice off as it formed.

Part way down we came upon an Eskimo and his outfit camped in the bush off to one side. We stopped in for a visit. He had his toboggan and dogs, and two caribou that had been killed on the other side of the height of the land. We discovered he was feeding his dogs seal meat, and when told that we would be interested to try some he invited us to help ourselves. What we saw lying in the snow beside his tent did not look very appetizing to say the least. The meat was bound with thick yellow blubber, and there was loose hair over the best part of it. When the seal meat runs low, he told us he would alternate the meat with a type of moss soaked in seal oil. We felt that this must surely be a dog's life.

Curly staking his claim at Sheep Creek in the Firth River Valley.

He gave us a fine big cut of caribou meat, and we arrived back at the camp for a festive evening. Fresh caribou meat! We had a mug of hot rum while the food was being prepared. Alex made several bannocks mixed right in the top of the flour sack. Curly cut up the caribou meat and fried it in bacon grease and this the five of us demolished with considerable relish.

Caribou is the most flavourful of all meat, wild or domestic. There is nothing to equal the savour of it when it is frying or the flavour of it when it is eaten. Oddly enough, it contains nowhere near the amount of nourishment to be found in moose or beef, but this is certainly mitigated by the excellence of the flavour. As a point of interest, the Canadian army operating in the north considers that the consumption requirement for each man of caribou meat is five pounds per day for proper nourishment.

The following day we rested, and then staked nine more claims on the Firth River itself above the mouth of Sheep Creek. In the initial rush the stakers had swung up Sheep Creek, leaving this ground still open.

Our journey back down to the original camp was not so tough an ordeal. We arranged with our Eskimo friend to take our packs down with his dogs and leave them on the river at the hairpin turn where the river swings back from the valley wall.

There was a Norseman aircraft in the valley when we arrived back, and five or six newcomers. Among them was Lon Philpot, who controlled most of the ground around the lower part of the river. Sunny Field was there, Jack Mulhulin, who had been Pool Field's partner, and there were several other businessmen from Aklavik.

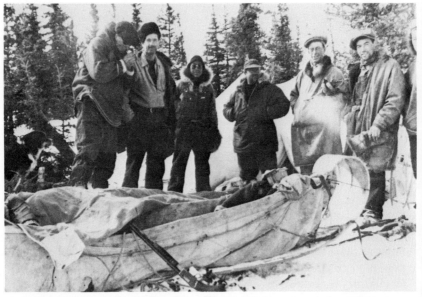

Left to right: Jack Mullhullin, the author, an Eskimo friend, Lon Philpott, Anchor Hoydle, Alex VanBibber, and Dick (Sunny) Field. Stampeders in the Firth River Valley.

We were tired when we arrived back, but decided to leave the valley as soon as possible while the weather held. The Norseman left immediately after discharging its load, and we felt we could not chance one more day. Spring was advancing. Clumps or mounds of grass, referred to as "nigger heads" were appearing as the snow melted and dried off rapidly in the continuous wind. If the weather closed in and held us there for too long a period we would not have enough snow on which to take off. We lit the blow pot, put it under the engine in the nose tent with the oil on top, and while everything warmed up we packed our gear over and loaded up.

The sky was overcast, the day dull, and there was a strong wind that came in powerful gusts. Our take-off path had to be of necessity along the bench parallel to the river, but it was generally into the wind. We felt we would still have time for our visit to the St. Roche before continuing on to Aklavik, and were looking forward to this with eager anticipation. A few moments after take-off we found it advisable to change our plan.

With the aircraft still tied to the ground we started up and warmed the motor to operating temperature. We then ran it up to full power, throttled back, and tested the magnetos at 1500 r.p.m. and found everything in order. Curly untied the wings, threw in the ropes and climbed in, we all fastened our seat belts and were ready to go.

The aeroplane pulled off the sticks which we left in the snow, and started the take-off run. The moment we became airborne the aircraft was carried rapidly to the left in a strong gust of wind, and we were headed straight towards the largest tree in the valley—a tree about as large as a good telephone pole and standing on the rim of the canyon. I tried desperately to get past it, and in the last moment put the right wing up to get it over the top, but it was not enough. We struck about six feet down from the top, at a point some four feet in from our wing tip.

One would imagine there would not be much time at this juncture and for a pilot in this particular situation to find his memory travelling back over the years to an incident that took place at the Royal Air Force Flying School at Medicine Hat, Alberta, in 1941, during the war.

Flying Officer "Windy" Winder was taking a load of airmen's boots to Lethbridge to be repaired, and he had his Air Speed Oxford Twin Engined Trainer loaded to capacity. He cleared for take-off with control tower, and then for some reason or other taxied to the wrong end of the runway so that in effect he would be attempting to take off down wind.

Taking off down wind is entirely possible as long as there is sufficient space in front to enable the aircraft to remain on the ground until flying speed is attained. Obviously, the advantage of taking off into the wind is that you can add the speed of the wind blowing against you to your ground speed and thus attain the air speed required for lift more quickly.

Windy had, no doubt, done his cockpit check while taxiing out, because he turned his aircraft onto the runway without stopping and headed for Lethbridge. We watched with fiendish glee when we realized what he was starting to do, never doubting for moment that he would be turned back by the tower.

Our amusement soon turned to dismay and then to horror as he persisted in his take-off run. Still on the ground he passed the end of the runway and headed across the prairie for Seven Persons Coulee. When he reached it his aircraft disappeared over the edge. We waited for a crash and a pall of smoke, and jumped on the crash tender as it headed across the drome.

It was not needed. A mile down the coulee we heard his engines, and there came the aircraft staggering into view above the edge of the prairie. He was a persistent man, Flying Officer Winder; he kept right on and delivered the boots to Lethbridge.

This escapade of Windy's turned from a moment of horror in the space of a few seconds to an incident which afforded us all considerable amusement and delight. As he recounted it, he had not taken off at all—he fell off!

He had persisted in his take-off run in the expectation of becoming airborne any second. Then as he hit the prairie the aircraft had slowed down a little but he had stayed right with it. When he went over the edge he was practically flying. He simply shoved the nose down into the coulee to get flying speed and had made a slight turn to fly along it. Once airborne, the aircraft gathered speed rapidly and he was on his way.

At the moment our wing hit the top of the tree and the Firth River Canyon was there below, the escapade of Flying Officer Winder crossed my mind. We had slewed around to the right but still managed to get the nose down into the canyon, regained a speed of fifty-five miles per hour which was, but only just, flying speed.

It was quite a ride and for a moment we were okay. We had, however, a further complication which would not have mattered too much had we not been so far away from anywhere.

An aircraft engine such as we had, attains, at full power, a maximum engine speed of about 3,400 revolutions per minute, which is permissible only for three minutes at the outside. It is available for take off. Normally after becoming airborne the r.p.m. are reduced to 2700, which is climbing power. This is accomplished by altering the pitch of the propeller, or by easing back the throttle if the propeller is fixed-pitch. Then again at the required height the revs are brought back to 2400 for cruising power.

We were at full power, and at this point as the aircraft gathered speed the aeromatic propeller should have adjusted itself to a coarser pitch, thus reducing the high r.p.m. of the motor. The fact that it did not was due, no doubt, to the damping fluid in the mechanism of the propeller being in a thickened heavy state from the cold and the prop would not respond as it should have; and as the revs would not come down automatically, I was compelled to throttle back to bring the tachometer needle back to a safe position on the dial. Twenty-seven hundred r.p.m. in full fine pitch gave us flying speed, but no more, and we could not climb out of the canyon so we flew along in it.

We were 200 miles from Aklavik and a further 600 or more to base. It seemed to be the best expedient to save the engine from damage, and the prop should react any second. We flew in the canyon at fifty-five miles an hour until we saw the hairpin turn ahead. It would not be possible, I knew, to get around the bend in the canyon. There was only one way to go, and that was up and over the edge.

We seemed to get lifted out by an up-draft, were again carried sideways, but at the same time we had gained enough height to shove the nose down again and turn into the canyon on the far side of the bend. Away we went—still in full fine pitch and the motor throttled back to safe r.p.m.

Neither Alex nor Curly said a word as we continued down the canyon making slight turns to correspond with the bends in the river. We went past the place where the new arrivals were gathered on the flat above to the left. They could hear us go by but could not see us, and certainly must have wondered what was going on.

Eventually the canyon petered out, and as we began to be able to see above the rim the propeller took hold and we could fly normally again.

We had no idea of the extent of the structural damage to the right wing. There was a piece of fabric flapping around on the under side of the wing that we could see, but that was all. The important thing was that we were still flying and we felt that we should stay flying until we reached Aklavik.

And so we missed our visit with the R.C.M.P. vessel, St. Roche. We went over the horseshoe bend, down to the coast, and back to Aklavik without further incident.

On the ground again at Aklavik, an examination of the wing showed the leading edge broken in as far as the main spar. The noses of two ribs were bent in, and the fabric was torn along underneath. This was fixed temporarily with a piece of tin, a piece of fabric and some dope provided by Mike Zubko. It was necessary to warm everything up with a Herman Nelson heater in order to be able to work with the dope in the cold air on the river bank, but it was managed satisfactorily.

The weather closed in as was anticipated, and grounded everything for a matter of eight days, so we fixed the aircraft and busied ourselves until we could get away.

Trappers were starting to leave for their camps on the delta; but many were still in Aklavik and there were several poker games in the large bunk houses in town to occupy the evening. A wise gambler, however, always quits when he is ahead!

It was pleasant travelling back along the route we had come, and we found our way over the unmapped portion of the route and into the Seela Pass without difficulty. Once, in the area of the Wind River the motor sputtered and the revs dropped alarmingly for a few seconds. Immediately we selected a safe landing place, and after circling it for a minute or two without further trouble, continued on our way.

At Dawson it was definitely spring. The strip on the river in front of the town was no longer in use, so we landed in slush at the airport, where our skis left a dark trail in the wet snow. It was necessary to refuel, etc., so we stayed the night. It was a good evening as everyone was anxious to learn of the goings on at the Firth stampede.

A telegraph to Whitehorse confirmed that there was still enough snow packed hard with rollers on one of the taxi strips, and although ski flying had been washed out on the drome we were permitted to proceed. We rose early to take advantage of the crust on the slush and the frozen grass, and managed to get off the ground before reaching the barbed wire fence. We circled back over the tailings on the Klondike River and headed for home.

It was a queer feeling to be flying an aircraft equipped with skis over a country from which the snow had gone. It was interesting, nevertheless, to note how much farther the spring had advanced as we continued south. Gradually the rivers showed less and less ice until there was none at all. And then we saw ducks and geese on the water and on the wing, ostensibly headed north, while we were coming south on skis.

At Whitehorse, wheels were fixed to the aircraft skis before we could get off the drome and into the hanger.

At Dawson we recorded the claims we had staked. The mining recorder then gave us metal tags that we were told must be taken back and attached to each one of the stakes!

We start our trek up the Firth River to stake claims on Sheep Creek.

Witch Country Tales

Happy Norman

Witch Country
Tales

The Nahanni Valley has always held a particular fascination for me because of the weird tales that are told in connection with it. And so I subsequently fell under the spell of Eugene J. Norman (Happy Norman), possibly one of the most unique and fascinating story tellers ever to be met. The last time I saw him was in 1952 when he was 93 years old, still hale and vigorous and his old happy self.

We had met initially in 1946 in Quesnel, which at that time was the end of steel on the Pacific Great Eastern Railway. I still have his card, "Specialist in Placer Mining and Glacier Channel Geology, Alaska, Yukon, British Columbia, 40 years Field Experience".

We made several trips together during that spring break-up, with back packs and snowshoes, and it was a wonderful experience to get out in the bush with the old chap who had spent the best part of his life north of '60. The 60th parallel of latitude is the northern boundary of the Canadian provinces.

On our first night in the bush, we stopped an hour before dark to make camp, and by the time it was dark we had everything at hand for our needs, and a comfortable camp for the night. With a knowing eye he selected a sheltered area by the stream we had been travelling, and his reasons for the selection became apparent as we went about the business of settling in.

The first consideration, was fire wood, and there close by was a large dead cotton wood girded with loose dry bark, heavily serrated and two or three inches thick. We soon broke loose the bottom part, which fell away with little or no effort, and by the time he had cut a long willow and shoved it up under the loose parts that we could not reach, we had it all off to about 20 feet. In another 20 minutes I had a pile about five feet long and three feet high, neatly stacked between two trees close to the fire place. It amazed me how, when it fell, most of the bark broke into pieces the size of stove wood, and the larger pieces were soon reduced to this size without even the use of an axe.

Next he took his small, long handled, double-bitted axe, which he carried shoved in his belt and which he had firmly requested me not to use under any circumstance, and quickly felled, leaning away from the camp, a green spruce that was roughly sixteen inches through. "With ma hax I make a stove", he said. And sure enough, with two six-foot logs from this tree lying parallel about a foot apart, we had a fire place where we could cook with hot bark at one end and have a fire for light at the other end.

There was special wood for cooking, another type for light, and yet a third type of fire wood that had the characteristic of burning without throwing sparks, and this was used for the evening fire and spared us the annoying business of having our sleeping bags burnt full of holes.

For supper we had thick-sliced fried bacon, and after the bacon was cooked and laid out on the clean bark of one of the logs, Happy quickly mixed up some batter which he cooked in the bacon grease. The thick batter rose up into fluffy bannock, crisp on both sides. We had three small bannock each, two with bacon laid between the crusts, and one with honey—all of which made a delicious and satisfying supper. This in turn was rounded off with a couple of mugs of hot tea. There is just nothing that beats the flavour of tea that is made out over the open fire. The billy can for the tea hangs on the end of a green pole, sharpened at the butt and shoved into the ground, preferably under some roots, and propped up with a stone or chunk of wood so that the can hangs at the proper height above the fire. When the water boils and the tea is dropped in, it is allowed to boil for a few seconds before being shoved to one side to steep.

There were no dishes to wash. It is true we each had a plate, bowl, cup, and knife, fork and spoon. Between us we had a couple of pots, a frying pan, a billy can, a small jar to hold the excess grease and the gold pan for the wash basin; but we only used the frying pan, one bowl, a couple of mugs and a spoon. The frying pan was left upside down on the snow, and the rest were rinsed by the edge of the partly opened stream.

The purpose of our trip was to re-stake a five-mile placer lease on this particular gold-bearing stream. He showed me the oxidization in the cut banks which had indicated mineralization and had encouraged him to investigate the placer possibilities of the stream.

We found his test holes 10 to 15 feet deep and about 4 feet square, and as it was in gravel they were roughly cribbed with cut poles.

In order to find the true values in placer ground it is necessary to sample the gravel all the way to bed rock, and of course it is always at the bottom where the best values lie. The hole is tested every foot or so all the way down, and he explained that while making his investigations along this particular stream he had paid himself wages at the rate of $15.00 a day from the sale of the gold he recovered.

Eventually he would lease the creek to a company that would put a dredge on it. He would receive so much as an initial payment, and thereafter a royalty of 5% or so of the gold recovered.

We located the old stakes and put up new ones which we placed beside the old.

During this time, 1946, there had been a resurging interest in the Nahanni Valley, the fabled area in the Northwest Territories out of which tales had come of headless corpses, fierce natives in a tropical setting, and streams rich with placer gold. And so it was of this valley that we talked as we sat by the fire during the evenings on our trip.

He was born in Fort Norman in the Northwest Territories, around 1859. This fur trading fort had been founded by his grandfather, Urik John Norman, in the year 1812. His forebears were Eskimo, Indian, Scottish and French. He spoke with a marked French accent, and knew most of the native dialects across the North, including Eskimo.

His first venture into the valley had been at the age of fourteen, when he accompanied his brothers on a spring beaver hunt. The route from Fort Norman in those days was up the MacKenzie River to the Keele River, and thence up the Keele to its source on Mount Christie where the head waters of the Nahanni River also have their origins. The dog teams were then headed eastward down the Nahanni to a point where they crossed over to what was then known as the Little Nahanni and what is now named the North Nahanni, and so on to the MacKenzie again and down north to Fort Norman and home.

As a boy on these trips it was his responsibility to carry the fire, smouldering in the inside filament of a hard tree fungus. They cut a flap and lay it back on the fungus, and a hot coal and some blowing soon transferred the fire to the fungus where it smouldered away under the flap until it was required again.

In former years his father had built cabins along the route, and in the area where the cross-over was made to the Little Nahanni he found Mucovite Mica in sheets large enough to be used for windows in the cabin.

Naturally, his knowledge of the area expanded as the result of many journeys through the valley and his constant association with the Indians, and he told of many of the truths out of which have sprung the fascinating tales one hears in connection with this fabulous "Headless Valley".

Happy spoke of the McLeod brothers, whose headless bodies were found in their camp, and of how this occasion caused the Nahanni to become known as the "Headless Valley"—a dubious appellation that still persists. Added to this incident, were others no less seemingly fantastic, that added still more substance to the stories connected with this fabulous place.

He explained that the McLeod brothers, trappers and prospectors, had been warned many times by those whose only place of existence could be the "witch" country to which they had been banished. Naturally they were jealous of the only country available to them, of the fur to be taken; nor did they want an influx of men who would come to wash gold from the streams.

Certainly the McLeod boys had been murdered and their heads had been missing when they were found, but there was also talk of a third man who had been with them, and who subsequently made his way alone from the valley and paid his way, when he reached the outposts, with gold dust.

Other camps had been found during the years containing the bones and equipment of other men, gold seekers mostly, who, leaving the outposts, headed into or through the valley carrying their groceries—bacon, beans, and flour—on their backs. Many of these men, not possessed with the skills or the knowledge that would enable them to live in a state of good health off the country, had frequently perished from scurvy.

The camps were located close to water because as their bodies grew weaker and more lethargic they had required water without having the strength to carry it any distance. When the skulls had not been carried off by animals and could be found, there was always the indisputable evidence of scurvy indicated by the fact that there were no teeth in the skulls. If the camp had not been too greatly disturbed, the teeth and even finger nails could often be found.

He explained that when the skull of a man is found and scurvy had not been the cause of death, the teeth are more firmly fixed in the shrunken bones of the jaws than they had ever been in life.

Men have since learned that life cannot be sustained by a steady unvarying diet of salty bacon, beans, and flour and that even when it is possible to obtain wild meat some must be eaten raw, some cooked, and a good portion of the viscera should be consumed as well. It is in the liver, kidneys, etc. that the vitamins and other elements required by the body are found. While he did not suggest that an animal's eyes should be eaten, he drew my attention to the fact that the eyes are the first things taken from a carcass by crows and other carrion eaters.

When an Eskimo, whose diet is usually straight meat or fish, makes a kill, the first thing he wants is the tongue. Then he goes for the liver, heart, kidneys, parts of the stomach, intestines, the rib cage, the brisket, and generally the front end of the meat. This part of the animal, while being meat of a coarser texture, is sweeter and full of rich flavour.

The animal's brain too is sometimes eaten, but as it has a quality that is indispensable to the tanning of the hide it is generally saved for this purpose.

An interesting departure from a civilized preparation of meat consists of the use of a combination of front-end meat and viscera. Here the last fourteen inches of the large colon is removed, turned inside out and thoroughly washed. This part of the animal is known as the "bum gut". After having been washed it is turned back to right side out again and filled with a strip of fatless meat usually from the neck. The ends are then tied off and the whole is very slowly roasted near to the hot coals of the camp fire, where it picks up a touch of smoke to add to the flavour.

Happy spoke also of the preparation of pemmican which is a mixture of dried meat, dried berries and grease. Both the meat and the berries are dried and reduced to a coarse powder. This in turn is packed in a grease-lined skin bag, grease is poured in over the top, the bag drawn together, and the whole thing is buried and the place marked. He told me that travelling over large areas of the Yukon and Northwest Territories he could still direct himself to areas and locate the sites where he knew there would be a pemmican buried.

For the greater part of his life he lived from eating, as he noted, "hard foods";

and while at the age of 90 he still possessed all his teeth, they were worn down completely to the gums. He could strike a match where there appeared to be no teeth at all.

Here was a man indeed who exemplified the proposition that a mixture of races produces what is known as "hybrid vigour". Here was a man of 90 who would head for the bush for four days, travel on snowshoes carrying a forty-pound pack, and still have the incentive and the energy to play a few tricks on his younger companion. My pack, which he had insisted on packing, had 15 pounds of rocks in the bottom, which I carried all day and discovered the first night out—a thing which afforded him endless delight when I discovered it, and in the telling of it thereafter when we arrived back.

The time of year was very early spring, and there was a considerable depth of snow still in the woods. As a consequence we travelled for the most part on snowshoes.

On our feet we wore shoe packs as it was starting to thaw during the day, and we carried our snowshoes hung on our packs until we were required to use them. It was then that I learned how to fasten on the snowshoes with a "squaw hitch" using a lamp wick for ties, and discovered that by using this type of fastening it was not necessary to bend down to put the snowshoes on or take them off after tying them initially.

The first thing to learn is to watch for willows that guide your advancing snowshoe inward so that is comes down on the edge of the other shoe. By this time your weight and balance are already forward and, as you cannot pick up your back foot to put it down ahead, down you must go. Then you find the ground, on which you want to put your hands to help you up, is out of reach under four feet of snow, so it is a difficult time especially with a pack on your back.

Happy told me of the last time he had trapped in the Nahanni, during the winter of 1924-25. That year he had taken his furs to Portland, Oregon, and sold them for twice what he would have received at a trading post in the north. While enroute back to Dawson in the Yukon with 40 head of horses, he and his partner had over-nighted with their stock in Calgary, Alberta.

During the evening of course, they had sought entertainment in the company of some ladies whose establishment catered to the requirements of men seeking such entertainment. His friend had gone back home to the hotel earlier than he, and had left in time to escape being quarantined in the establishment for a matter of three weeks on account of measles or some such malady. Apart from the time he lost, there was something of a bill at the stockyards for three weeks' board for 40 head of horses.

He showed me a ragged scar across his abdomen that had been made by a German bayonet during the 1914-1918 war. He had a few other scars—teeth marks and claw marks acquired during moments of carelessness that were bound to have occurred during his long years of trapping, hunting and prospecting north of '60.

He told me that as a younger man he had spent long hours with an old Indian woman, recording in French many of the events responsible for the dispersion of the various Indian tribes throughout the Canadian North. The notes containing this material, and other accounts of fabulous journeys and interesting happenings, I was unable to acquire because they had been willed to the Smithsonian Institute in Washington.

There were many things we talked about during our evenings in camp. Of the natural hot springs there, and of a coal seam that had been burning as a result of a lightning strike as far back as an old Indian, who had been a friend of his father, could remember. These two perfectly natural phenomena were, in the eyes of the Indians, very unnatural, and as a consequence the valley had for countless years been considered by the Indians as witch country and the place for banishment of renegade members of the tribe—those who had broken certain of the tribal laws, more particularly the laws that pertain to marriage.

In most primitive societies the system of family totems has been set up. It exists among the natives of Africa in exactly the same way it does among the North American Indians. The families of each tribe belong to larger families known as totems, and these are named after animals and birds, and sometimes fish. Across the Canadian North the two most numerous totems are the wolves and the crows, and the elders of the tribes are adamant in their enforcement of the ancient tribal law that a wolf may not marry a wolf, nor a crow marry a crow, not even from a far distant tribe.

And so, as it is with all laws, there are those who do not keep them, and the penalties must be exacted, and the penalty for breaking the marriage law was usually banishment for the male. For the woman it was slavery. She must, until the end of her days, do menial work about the camp or the village in return for her food and shelter.

Happy told me the story of such a happening. It had taken place when he was a boy, and he remembered it.

The girl had been ready for marriage the year past, but as her mother was dead, her father had kept her in his lodge because of her usefulness, and because of her increasing market value to him as a bride for the highest bidder. Her own interest were centered in her younger brothers and sisters.

The young man came from another area. He had been travelling for some days when there before him was a scene that froze his blood. A young woman and a boy picking berries, and beyond that a grizzly bear that had stalked to within a distance close enough to charge.

A grizzly bear is without question the most dangerous of all animals to encounter in its own element. Although its sight is poor, it has an exceptionally good sense of smell and of hearing. Its strength, speed, and vitality are beyond belief. It is unpredictable and possessed of a very crafty brain.

When it is said that he is unpredictable, it should be qualified by saying that he is more or less unpredictable—for it is known that when he is on a kill, or if a female has cubs that she thinks may be endangered—an attack is a certainty. The thing that is uncertain is the time and place, and it can be expected to come with a well calculated element of surprise.

A grizzly may leave the scene and never be seen again; or it may, having put the cubs into safety, return and wait beside the trail up ahead or suddenly appear from behind and charge.

It is the lord of all it surveys, and is required to back down from no living thing apart from another of its kind.

And so it was on this sunny day in the berry season the three parties were converged at the same spot. The girl and her young brother, berry picking; the grizzly bear, about to charge; and the young hunter equipped with bow, arrows and a spear.

At the same moment that he fixed an arrow to his bow-string, shouted and ran forward; the bear charged.

The young woman, when she became aware of the bear, sprang for the boy and covered him with her body, and as they went down a few lengths in front of the bear it received an arrow in the shoulder. It stopped, and turning its head to bite at the arrow, the grizzly was struck by a second arrow just back of the jaw below the ear. There was a third arrow knocked on the string and ready to fly, but the second arrow had done its work effectively, cutting the jugular, and as the blood pressure was released from the bear's brain its world went black and down it went to thrash out ineffectively the last of its great strength.

These were the circumstances under which they met. But they were both of the same totem.

The man returned to his people, but he could not stay, and journeyed back. Together, they disappeared.

For two years they lived apart from the ken of their people, but their world was not large enough to hide them forever, and once an indication of their whereabouts became known they were hunted down and brought back to appear before their people.

The law is the law—inflexible. For the man—banishment to the Nahanni Witch Country; for the woman—slavery.

Yukon Epics

Ira Van Bibber

Yukon Epics

Some of Ira's family with part of a winter's fur catch. From left to right: George, Dode, Lucy, Linch, Archie, Michael, Short, and Ira. The boys have just recently returned from the war overseas.

Ira VanBibber was a marvellous story-teller, and could keep his listeners spellbound during the course of many an evening whenever the opportunity afforded a visit with him.

A year or two before he died in 1965, he visited my home with Mrs. Van Bibber, and we settled down with some home brew for an evening of yarns. This was what he loved best, and because he enjoyed himself so thoroughly he was, as is always the case, extremely good at it. It is unfortunate that his voice, his chuckles and his laughter are lost when the stories are written down but this cannot be helped.

In appearance he was tall, gray-haired and undoubtedly had been a powerful man in his younger days. He was softly spoken, and his manner was courtly and gentle.

Like many men of his generation, he set great store by a man's ability to cuss in a good round fashion. The display of such a wondrous talent in a man inevitably afforded him great amusement. He always maintained to me that when he died and was being buried, he did not need to have missionaries or preachers officiating his funeral. What he would like, he said was to have one of his good friends stand by the graveside and give him a good cussin' out in a loud voice. I would have liked very much to have heard either him or one of his friends in an exhibition of cussin' but I never did.

He was born and raised in the mountains of West Virginia, a "ridge runner"...he said. He came west to become a cowpoke, but "got throwed off a horse" so he tried logging, and when that life did not appeal to him, he and his brother landed in Skagway with the gold seekers at the turn of the century.

Because of their size and strength, the brothers were hired by "Whiskey" Sullivan to pack $50,000 worth of liquor over the pass and on to the gold fields at Dawson.

In the Yukon, he found his Utopia and with his wife "Shorty" trapped, traded, hunted, and raised a large family centered at Pelly Crossing.

He had two separate partners in those early days, Dell Van Gorder was the first, and then later when Dell settled down and became a trader for the pioneer merchants Taylor and Drury, he teamed up with George Steel.

Dell Van Gorder was also a big man both physically and in stature among the old-timers. I met him at Ross River in 1948 when he ran the T & D post there and at that time was impressed by his fine appearance and quiet manner.

Van Gorder also took a native wife and had a family of five children, but he lost them all and his wife as well to tuberculosis. Eventually he married again and settled at Teslin, where he died shortly after. Both Van Bibber and Van Gorder, had many adventures together, and Ira laughingly related to me of the time they were trapping up in the Pelly Lakes. They picked a 30 gallon barrel of berries. They put sugar in with it; but naturally they didn't have enough with them to make a good job, and it was sour. Ira tells it better than I do; "Well, we drank it; it was good for awhile, but it went flat, you know, and, uh, Van Gorder says, 'Now', he says, 'it's a shame we got to throw that away.'

"I says, 'We won't throw that away', I says.

"'Well', he says, 'what will you do with it?'

"I says, 'We'll run it off in liquor', I says.

"'Well now, what are you goin' to use for runnin' it off?'

"And I says, 'We got a good shot-gun here and a lot of moulds for makin' candles, do you see?'

"We took those candle moulds and butted them together and put it on the shot gun, and there we had our still. We butted them candle moulds together and took dough and wrapped around it, and as soon as that baked a little it was solid then, you know. Yes, sir, we run her off then.

"I was telling Van Gorder—ohhh, it was awfully cold weather—and I was telling Van Gorder, 'now you stay in the house,' I said, 'or if you go out,' I said, 'don't get down.' So he was ginned up with the fumes of that liquor in there, you see.

"So he went out and turned all the dogs loose, and he lay down kickin' and playin' with the dogs and he couldn't get up to save his neck, no, sir! He crawled up and I had to help him up to get him in, you know. You don't know you're drunk either, that's the funny thing about it.

"Talkin' of liquor," Ira said almost in the same breath, launching into another tale, did you ever hear of old 'Whiskey' Sullivan? He was a logger from the coast. He came in here and made a strike, and made $50,000. He went outside and laid it out in liquor and landed in Skagway with it. I was there. I didn't have no money and was hoboin' my way into the Klondike, and you had to have a stake to get in—a thousand pound of grub. And so he came up to me, this big man did, and put his hand on my shoulder, just lightly, you know, and he says:

"Excuse me for being so familiar,' he says, 'but didn't I see you talkin' with a big feller down there yesterday, or maybe the day before? Maybe you noticed me walk by?

"And I did, too; he was a giant of a man himself.

"I said, 'yes', I said.

"'You know him?' he says.

"I says, 'yes', I says.

"'Do you think a feller could get that feller?'

"And I says, 'I guess so' and I says, 'What do you want?'

"'I got some packin' to do over the pass,' he says, 'and he just looked like he could pack a horse load.'

"You see, he was six feet seven, my brother; he was a giant of a man.

"So anyway he hired the two of us to pack over the White Pass. Yes, sir, here's the way he done it. He laid that out in liquor—he laid that mostly in alcohol—'Twasn't liquor at all.

"Then he went to Vancouver and got himself a blender, and blended all that up into the kind of liquor he wanted—scotch, rum, rye and everything like that. He made an immense fortune with liquor and then he put that in and bought three steam boats and went boatin' and went broke, and then he went to the lower river.

"In 1912, I was workin' in Dawson on the dredges and this man come up and cuffed me from behind. I was workin' the night shift, and I was off by the fires—it was a frosty mornin', and I was hoverin' over the fire after breakfast—and so I looked up, and there was old Whiskey Sullivan.

"'What are you doing here?' I said.

"'I'm a hired carpenter,' he said.

"I says, 'What did you do with all that money?'

"'Got her,' he says.

"I said, 'How much of it?'

"'Well me and my partner had 80 head of horses down in Alaska,' he said, 'We were pretty well broke,' he says, 'and I skipped out to get a job of work,' he says.

"Now isn't that the damndest thing? I never seen or heard of him since you know.

"Yes, sir, $50,000 we packed it over that pass. Well, you see, we didn't need a grub stake then, we was working! And he didn't want to fire us, do you see, and the police couldn't make him fire us, so we worked right on through and went to Dawson. Yes, sir, that was the way I came into the Yukon."

"I had an idea that you came in through the Nahanni," I ventured, "but you came up over the White Pass."

"No, I went into the Nahanni from this side. I spent three years around Selkirk. And there's where I met Shorty, in Selkirk.

"The way I met Shorty, me and my partner had a tradin' outfit, and we were gettin' ready. We threwed all our stuff out of the cabin and segregatin' the stuff we wanted to take with us and hauled it down to the boat, and put the other stuff back in the cabin, you see. We were busy takin' care of the stuff there, and here come this old woman.

"Of course, we had been acquainted with the Indians there, and we knowed them all, but this one was a stranger. Here she come with a kid on her back and a couple of them followin' along, just behind was a little, oh my gosh you'd be surprised, a nice little...and I noticed her right away. So then I asked her 'do gee?' What's your name? the more I asked her, 'do gee?', the more she would giggle. Well, that was all right.

"Then goin' up the Pelly, I thought of her a time or two, you know. Well naturally I would. I was a young feller then. Then we got out to the lake, Tatlmain Lake and started fallin' timber to build a cabin and get a place ready and in shape, and we looked over and there come two girls. That's the time we got acquainted, yes sir.

"That's a long time ago, yes, sir, long time ago. And I haven't been sorry. No, sir, if anybody's spent a happy life, I have. When we come out of the hills in that Nahanni country—up in that country—oh my! You see, there was fur and then we was havin' children, and we took a boy 14 years old with us—he growed up, you see, and became a man—and that's all that we needed to have company. But when it come down to business, we liked to get out in the hills where we were free, do you see. Go anywhere we liked—greatest life in the world, you know. We trapped and that was the way we made our money, and there was plenty of game. It was a wonderful life with Shorty.

"But don't think she hasn't worked in her day. When that skin was taken from the moose's back and throwed to her, she took that skin and tanned it and made it into mocassins and clothes for the little ones. She made clothes of all kinds, and that takes work. Fourteen youngsters we raised to men and women, do you see. That's a lot of kids. She's worked in her time now.

"I was just thinking", he continued after a brief interruption..."I can't understand what's going on...Now, I was travelling through the country, and I came to a canyon, a deep canyon, swift water. It was getting towards fall, very low water. I was tellin' old Wilson about this, where I was comin' through. We was talking about the country and he had been in there himself, too. So I was telling him that at the foot of that canyon there, that it was the prettiest sight yet, I said, 'that peacock copper', I said, 'with the sun shinin' on it—you know how those blues would look with the sun shinin' on it.'

"'Peacock copper, hell!' he says, 'You never saw no peacock copper, there's none there.'

"He says, 'That was silver,' he says, 'that was gelena' he says, 'I walked across the dyke above that', he says, 'and looked like it was pretty near pure silver', he says.

"And so it was the same canyon then, and Dan, my oldest boy, made two trips up there and never found the canyon—now what do you think of that? What went wrong?

"I remember when Danny was going up there, and he was wanting me to fly him in there," I said "and Alex talked to me about it at the same time. That would be about six years ago."

"Why is it? What went wrong? What's the matter?"

"Well, I guess it's still there."

"And now this big Ole, you know..."

"Yes, Ole Rollag."

"Yes, well, he said last spring..he was up there and saw it from a flyin' machine, but he said he couldn't reach it. But why is it that Dan didn't find it when he was up there; according to old Wilson—old Wilson's worked in the silver mines out in Montana and through here, you know ..."

"Is that the Wilson that runs the cement block outfit here in town?"

"No, no, no, this is an Indian. He used to be up in the upper country there. He never come into civilization. Oh, he got through to Mayo; he lived around Mayo, but he kept out in the woods. He'd killed a couple of fellers and was on the dodge, do you see? He made the same trip, he told me. He says, 'I struck the canyon just like you did.' He come down there to the mouth and waded the creek travellin' the same way.

"And then she (Shorty) and I and this little Indian that was with me, we made the same trip across there and struck the canyon, but we cut a tree across the canyon, and there's something that scares me every time I think of it too, by golly! I can't even keep from being nervous about it.

"We cut that tree and packed the dogs one at a time over with the packs on— didn't unpack them, you know—and then we come for her; but she wouldn't buck that, you know, she was afraid of it. So I got sore, and I just picked her up in my arm and walked over there with her. Wasn't that the craziest thing a man ever did! And I couldn't see this log down there because I held her out in front, you know. I packed her over there, and you know, it still kind of scares me to think of it. I had great nerve, I guess. Must of had—to do a trick like that.

"Well now, Van Gorder and I must have had great nerve. The Indians was tellin' us about runnin' the canyon below Virginia Falls there in the Nahanni. We swore that if the Indians had done it we could do it. We went in there and run that canyon, you know. That was the most dangerous thing, do you see. There would be swift water, rough water, and then you'd come into slack water.

"And there'd be these rolls...them rolls would come up higher than this ceiling. If one of them rolls caught the boat, why you'd be done, of course. You just had to dodge around them, you know.

"And we run that, and Van Gorder, when he was down in that—you couldn't explain the noise hardly it was makin'—Van Gorder says, 'This is, I never expected to be in hell,' he says, 'but I guess we're here right now,' he says. Yes, sir, we were real nervous. Well, a two-skin boat—two hides on an eight-foot frame, you see—but that was the best thing you could have was that little boat, you see."

I asked him, "What did you use for a gun in those early days, a 30-30, a 44-40?"

"No, a 30-40 altogether," Ira replied.

"Black powder?"

"No, no, used smokeless. The smokeless guns come out about the time of the first 30-40's we bought, do you see...Before we got the 30-40, we loaded our own shells with black powder. The 45-70 and 50-55 made a helluva big cloud of white smoke. You had to wait till it cleared away to see what you had shot.

"Talk about a smoke, makes me think of, we were goin' to take Christmas with porcupine to eat, is all we had to eat now; and so I said to Shorty—and oh, cold!—what was wrong, we couldn't get any meat on account of the cold weather, you know, you can't hunt in the cold weather. The wolves drove the moose back; and no moose, no nothing. Porcupine; and we were out in the McCarthy Mountains here. And so, in the morning I was feeling pretty wicked to put my family on a dinner of 'day daw', they call porcupine. I told Shorty, 'I'm goin' huntin'.

"'Oh, no, it's too cold. Wait it out,' she says.

"No, sir, I started out, and I got up on what we call a hog's back...it made a dip and went up on to the main mountain. And comin' up here was a bunch of sheep. I didn't know there was sheep in that mountain because the wolves had chased them out, and they chased them out along that ridge. I guess that's the reason they happened to be out there, and they were comin' off.

"I sneaked up, and when they was crossin' this low place, I got just as close as I could when they come down—when they went any further they would be goin' away from me. Well, when they come down there—and oh, cold, you know—I dodged under the smoke from my breath and shot and knocked one down.

"Now they went out and up on the bluff there and stood up, and it was a llloooonnnggg shot, but I said, 'I'm goin' to waste a shell on you anyway,' I had to duck under my breath once more; I fired, and that one rolled over. Yes, sir, two; and they were fat ewes, too. I pulled the insides out of one of them and let it lay there, and took the other one and headed for home, you know, and took it right in the cabin and dressed it. We had the best Christmas dinner we ever had. Yes, sir, luck was with us—that was a lucky day."

"The one you left up there, you took the insides out and left it lay?" I asked.

"Oh, yes, left it lay. Stretched it out so it would drag easy. If you left the insides in they would spoil overnight, do you see. It would sour. Oh, yes, any big animal wants to be pulled or drawed, you know.

"It's awful dangerous. Van Gorder was huntin' with the Indians, you know, and it was cold weather, and they finally killed three big bulls. They dressed out two of them, and the other they just left it lay with the insides still in it. Over a period of time they cooked the best of these two, what they figured was the best, you know, and they ate that.

"Then they moved camp, and Van Gorder was tellin' me he went out and chopped some of the meat out of that frozen one there, for dog feed. Skookum Charlie went with him, and Charlie took a bunch of meat for dog feed but when he got to camp, he cut out a pot of it and put it to cookin'. Van Gorder said he begged him not to eat that. No, sir, he ate it and took sick. Ptomaine poison 'twas what it was, you see.

"And when I come down in the spring, I was askin' Van Gorder what was wrong with Charlie. Oooh, poor fellow. He looked awful, you know. So he was tellin' me this story; and anyway, I think he died about that time when we come down there, if not later on. Anyway it killed him.

"Oh, that ptomaine poison! There's two poisons, two types of decayed meat. You take meat that's soured, it goes all through it. And even if the insides is pulled and it heats, why that is what you call sour. Then another kind of decayed meat is where it is started on the outside after it is cooled through. You can cut that bad part off, and the inside of that's good, you see, no danger of poison there. But if that's poisoned through and through, that's dangerous then. Most of the Indians are very careful of that.

"But they will eat this meat on the outside that's tainted, and thrive on it, you know. 'Twon't hurt them a bit. But that that's soured, that's not good for you, no, sir. It pays a feller to be careful, you know.

"Yeh, it's amusing. Steel and I, we thought we were hunters, but we really didn't know good meat. You see, after an animal runs out, it's not fit to eat. It's not good meat at all. We'd kill an old poor bull or a ram sheep and eat of that, you know, and we thought we were just livin' fine.

"One day, the dogs run three rams into a cliff and held them there, and we come down and shot them. And at the side of the glacier there was water runnin' along nice, and we started a fire and cut steaks of that and roasted it on a stick by the fire; and Steel filled up on that, you know—he was hungry. He went out, and he laid down, and he took a big drink of water. 'Now', he says, 'when you can go out and kill your game and eat a feed of it and take a drink of water and satisfy, then,' he says, 'you're all right.' It wasn't fit to eat, you know. We didn't know."

Later, Ira spoke of a lesson he had learned in raising his enormous family of 14 children, and that story rolled on into another.

"If you have any sense at all you'll never lick a boy," he said. "You know my oldest boy; it was at night time I give him a paddlin'. The Indians were camped just below, and old McGinty, he came right up.

"You'll see, you'll see," he says, 'that's not right,' he says. 'Some day you'll be sorry for that,' he says, 'You licked that boy,' he says, 'that's not right' he says, 'because don't ever lick a child,' he says. And he's right, too, you know. Well, I got to thinkin' about that. Well, I just turn them over to Shorty. She had her way and spared me some.

"If you can refuse them something that they want, do you see, that's what hurts. Now Danny and Abe was doin' some meanness, and I told them to quit. They kept right on and paid no attention to me, you know. I said, 'boys', I said, 'you'll see', I said, 'the next time we go to the fish net,' I said, 'and have a good time in the boat,' I said, 'you boys won't go.'

"Well, they went on and paid no attention, and tittered at me, I guess. I don't know. Anyway, we run the net about every two hours, plenty of fish comin', you know. So I said to Archie, 'it's time to run the fish net,' I said; so I started out, and Archie, he started walkin' right close behind me, and Abe and Danny come trailin' back. And Archie looked back; 'Danny and Abe, you can't go with us. We's goin' to see the fish net,' and my God, you know, they had to turn back, and they didn't go either.

"Them boys listened to me the next time I told them to do anything, they listened to me. You refuse to take them anywhere, and you'll hurt them worse than a lickin' now.

"No sir, a kid's just like a dog. If you lick a dog, he's no good.'

"Oh, you've got to give them a bat once in awhile,' I offered.

"No. No, sir. Look, I had more fights over that...."

"Well, you can reason with a kid, but you can't reason with a dog. You've got to give him a kick in the backside once in awhile."

"No, but there's a way with a dog. In the south, you know, we never lick our dogs, oh, no. You can lick your wife, but not your dog...You see, when I was driving stage here—I run from Dawson to Skagway—and, of course, I would be given dogs of all kinds, and I had trouble, you see, with them, of course, until I got them straightened out. They caught on to me pretty fast though.

"But these no-good East Coast Canadians is tough, is the toughest, wildest, no-account men that a feller could run into—sailors, toughs—and they were all dog-men. They worked with Boris Priest. He used to run a bunch of men with dogs, the Arctic Express. You've certainly read about the Arctic Express, that was this express from Dawson to Skagway.

Pat and George ploughing with a dog team.

"Well, they hired all that riff-raff, you see, to drive the dogs. They had lots of dogs, and anyway, when they was passin' my team, they would give my dogs a cut with the whip, and them dogs bein' whipped would howl. Now let a hound dog howl. I was right around there to see what he was howlin' about; and one of them that hit that dog he got right into trouble; and, oh, I've got many a beatin' up now, there's no gettin' around it.

Linch and Lucy—summer travel with pack dogs.

"You could hardly lick one of them, they was such powerful men, you know. There was no weaklin' on that coast, you know. They was so cantankerous the weaklin's died off, and they're the only ones that was left. That's true now, I'm telling you the truth now, damn it!

"But I got back at them in Selkirk—they mutinied. Archie MacCarven—he died up on the Mayo country—he was superintendent of the Arctic Express, you see, and he got into Selkirk, and he had this bunch of East Coast Canadians there, all dog drivers, and handlin' the dogs, and they got to drinkin'.

"Archie didn't drink—he was a school teacher from out on the plains, and he had no business with the job that he had, do you see, he really didn't know nothin' about the job. Well, he made some remark or got into it, and they quit on him...and they took to drinkin' heavy.

"Now Price and Yonkins was in Selkirk at the same time with their loggin' crews, Mississippi loggers, and they was doin' a little drinkin' as well. Well, I was thinkin' there's goin' to be a fight and there sure was. They got into a fight there, and it was a hard fight, there's no gettin' around it.

"Now there was Belgian Joe—he died down there close to Dawson just a year or so ago—anyway, he and I and a feller called McFadden wouldn't fight. We had it in for those Eastern Coast Canadians, and we wouldn't fight. We let them fight it out, and they got licked, too. There was a big chance we could have turned the tide, you see, if we got in there and fought with them fellers."

"They were fighting these Mississippi loggers?"

"Yea, Mississippi loggers, and they were tough, too, you know, yes, sir!"

"I guess there were some pretty tough men in those days."

"Oh my gosh, yes, they were tough, you know. If they'd have took to guns like they did in the West, it would have been a mess; but they didn't, no. When a man got his dose, he would holler 'enough'. That's all there was to it, you see. He took his lickin' decently. Oh, my, such fellers. And swear! It would raise the roof!"

"I was thinking," he told me later, "get that recordin' machine and let me make a statement on the Indians here. I've never seen any statement made."

"You are being recorded now."

"Well, I'm going to tell you something...I come to the Yukon a young man, and I had lived in what we call a Christian country. Churches by the wholesale and plenty of prayer. People that prayed and went to prayer meetin's and just a big-mouthin' and long-tonguein' and a helluva fussin' and nothing done...where I come from, and, of course, way back in the mountains, you know.

"But I come to the Yukon, and when I struck the Yukon was the first real Christian that I met in my life—I'm tellin' you now, right now. Now you will decide with me when I tell you the kind of people I met in the Yukon.

"I met a people—he was born sinless, he lived clear through his life sinless, he would rather die than commit a sin. He prayed to his God, but not in words, do you see, not in words. The words were a chant, you see, not like the white man...And he died sinless. Then, in time to come, he didn't stay dead, you see, he believed he would come back to this earth. He would come back to this earth with a pure spirit. That's the idea of an Indian bein' honest in his wild state, is to have as pure a spirit as he can to hand on to his, to the next time he comes, you see. Now do you understand what I mean?"

"So they believe they will come back again...reincarnation."

"Well, he comes back again. They know from signs, the Indians know who that is. So they claim—I don't know. I'm not tellin' you that for the truth, but they seem to know the spirit. Now she's re-incarnated, you see; all Indians is re-incarnated, come back to this world again, you know. And by golly, it's a lot more sensible than the white man's religion. He dies, but he never does come back. They tell you all kinds of stories.

"But the Indian was so pure and genuine. He wouldn't hit another Indian, he wouldn't kill a dog, no sir, he didn't kill. It was the same as killin' a man, they'd say, that's what they always told me, always kind to a dog. Of course, a dog was really a part of them, you know. And always so kind to the old people as well.

"And, of course, they were so religious, you see, so what you would call Christian. Now, I don't want to use that word now, because they lived far more accordin' to the Christian way than the white man does. But because they was not acquainted with and borne down with Christian dogmas, do you see they called him a savage. Should have been the other way around.

"Now, old Hoffly. He wrote the life of a Yukon bishop, you see, a kind of a pamphlet he wrote, didn't amount to anything. And he was tellin' about the Indians—those savages, he called them every little way—those savages.

"Of course, that was for the English people, you see, that was why he wrote that. They would go over there and beg money from the English, you see, beg money for the church. I know this is hurtin' you a little, but that's true now."

"No. It's awful, the Indian was so gentle and good and those old churchmen, they used to make me disgusted. It was awful, you know. I know. I lived right there."

It was time for a bit to eat, and I suggested coffee, homemade bread and butter and head cheese. He said that when he was a boy in the mountains of West Virginia they called head cheese "souse", and I recalled that my grandmother also, from the north of England, had referred to it as "souse".

"Now, ramps,' he said, "did you ever hear of ramps? Now wait till I tell you about that. If you eat ramps and go into a house, you will drive everybody out. Oh, my gosh—ramps. In West Virginia, they enacted a law that you could not go into a court room if you had been eating ramps, they would fine you for contempt of court."

"What is it? Garlic?"

"It's a kind of wild onion. It's the awfullest thing, you know. They found out the name originates in Scotland—rampus—and they still have rampus festivals in West Virginia and Kentucky there now."

We spoke of the time we met in Dawson in 1948. His son Alex, and Curly Desrosier and myself were on our way north to the Firth River gold rush, and he mentioned that he had given Curly a big old Peterson pipe.

"Yeh," he said, "then later Curly was tellin' me that you were flyin' along in a canyon and came to a wall, and when it got closer he just shut his eyes up tight. That must have been kind of exciting. You must have figured your time had come.

"I figured my time had come once, I'll tell you. We had been trappin' beaver, and the Indians come along, and we had a talk with them. And we was askin' them about the middle fork of the Pelly, and they were tellin' us it was good, but that was a mistake. It was the north fork that was good, and the middle fork was a son-of-a-gun now and no foolin' about that.

"Well, I wouldn't start out with the family on account of I didn't feel right about it, you see, so me and Tommy took the little skin boat and run down to have a look at the river. Tommy was nervous, and I noticed it, you know. And I noticed that the mountain had broke away and come down over the valley and had made a canyon in there. There must be a canyon that the stream had broke through, do you see, but we paid no attention.

"We could hear the noise, too, and we come around a bend, and the water was runnin' just as swift as it could, and we couldn't back up because the sides come straight down to the water, you see. We come right into that chute zone and started down it.

"It was swift, and Tommy—there was a drop out of the side of the canyon, and it made a whirlpool in there—and Tommy started diggin' for the whirlpool. I don't know why he done that because he must have knowed that was wrong, you see. But I had to keep the boat level or it would turn over, and we come into that whirlpool just at the lower end.

"I was in the stern, and I hopped out onto a shelf and held the boat, and he got out, too, and there we could see out of the mouth of the canyon. It just looked like a graveyard to me, rollin' up there you see, new dug graves, the water was muddy.

"This is the end!" I figured. Don't you know that nothin' hurt me, only that I had taken that young Indian in there and destroyed his life. No, sir, it just seemed like that was the end. What was the use? So we got close together so we could talk—it was makin' such a noise in there, that roarin' of water, you know. So I got close to him, I said, 'Tommy', I said, 'we'll dig sideways,' I said.

"You see, if we run to the head of that whirlpool, there was water coming over a rock, you see, that would pour over you. So I says to Tommy to start digging out sideways and lift the boat, do you see, a little two-skin boat. So we started diggin' out sideways, and we got pretty well to the upper end of that whirlpool, and of course the whirl was catchin' the boat, but we could hold it by throwin' our paddles flat on the water, we could hold it.

"And so anyway, we got pretty well up to the upper end, and we come into the current comin' by; that current caught us and shot us right clear out of the mouth of that canyon. Just what we wanted—shot us clear out there into them graveyards.

"When we got into the graveyard, we just dodged around most of them ripples that was rollin' up. When we got below them, on one side was rough water, and no boat could stand it. And that rough water come down and crossed the river to the other side; but here was nice land, and, by golly, we run in there and landed.

"When I got out of that boat, I was so weak I could barely walk. Oh, I was a coward. I was scared to death, you know. I don't know how we ever lived to get out of that, you know. That was a pretty hard proposition."

"Do you recall the story about the time of the avalanche on the White Pass summit?"

"Yes, sir, I do. I wasn't there, but it was related to me by old John Durant. He was a Frenchman, he was there and this is the way he told it to me:

"'We were dere, make our camp, and we sleep and d'snow come down and cover me up. But I get out, and my two partner laying up dere, dey can't get out, I get up and dig dem out, and dey was glad to get out of dere. So we get d' snow off and get d' tent up again and go to bed. We are tired for bring our outfit up on d' trail, so we sleep late.

"'We got up so to fix our breakfast, and d' policeman come and open up d' tent and say you fellow come out now, he say, the big snow slide. What about d' big snow slide? Well, d' big snow slide has cover lots of people up, and we want you fellow to come down and go to work.

"'We didn't know about dis, so we hurry trough our breakfast dere, and we go down, and we know about where d' people is bury, so we start to dig dere. We dug out some men, and soon dey set up a big tent to put d' bodies in, and dey were all up dere.

"'Den dey take my sleigh before, so come d' time I want it back, and I go to d' big tent and start to go in. A policeman catch me, and say, no, sir, you don't go in dere, but I go in when I tell him about my sleigh. And I see my sleigh standing over dere, so I get d' sleigh. Den by d' door I talk to d' guard. We stand dere and talk for a minute or two about something dat was noting, and a young girl come along and say to d' policeman, 'you give me dat dere man.'

"'No,' he say, 'dos men going to lay dere, and we give dem decent burel,' he say.' ('Buriel', he meant. Ira explained, called it 'Burel'.)

"'I look at dat man, I see someting, I can't tell though what. He just don't look like a dead man, but I don't say anyting. So the policeman say, 'Okay you take him, sure, you take him. But if dat man is dead, you bring him back here.'

"'So I went back to my tent with my sleigh. When I get to Dawson, I see dat young fellow and dat girl walk togeder in Dawson.

"'I see dem walk togeder,' he says.

"And so anyway, I was talking to Tom Hibberd, Tom Hibberd knows everything, you see. I was asking Tom Hibberd about it. And Tom Hibberd says, 'Yes', he says, 'them people lived nine years up on Swede Creek above Dawson,' he says. "Yes', he says, 'that's a true story,' he says."

It would have been edifying to have spent an evening with Tom Hibberd before he took off for the last great stampede. He had been in Dawson virtually from the start and as Ira says, "he knew everything."

He was a witness to the contract where a miner, a Swede, bought a dance hall girl for her weight in gold. There are several versions of the story: One, that she went out to the creeks with him and then feigned illness, came into town and went back to enjoyin' life as she had known it. The other version was that she was actually ill and in the hospital and Tom Hibberd went up to see her. She told the doctor that she had to go back or lose her contract, and the doctor objected.

Tom told Ira that the Swede reached in his pocket, pulled out the contract and tore it up right there. He gave her the gold anyway, and she subsequently pulled out. Gold was plentiful in those days in Dawson.

We spoke of the Indian way of life in those early days. "Do you know how an Indian baby is born?" Ira said. "Well, it's a strange thing the way they lived; but when you think about it, it's all very natural and fittin' for the circumstances they found themselves in.

"That baby is dropped right on the brush. You see, they jerk the blanket out from under the mother so it won't get soiled, and that youngster is born on the brush—think of that. Then it's picked up, and the cord is cut and tied and everything, and it's wrapped up and handed a tit. That's the way they come into the world. Strange and interesting thing.

"This girl, she was havin' trouble, you see, with her baby, and the Indian men were all away to get meat. And oh, cold, son-of-a-gun it was cold! But anyway, we come almost to where the men was supposed to meet us. These two old women, they knew that her time had come and they was supposed to take care of her. And we was all hungry, no meat, do you see. So we left these two old women and the giri and went on to make camp.

"Anyway, these two old women claimed that the girl wouldn't work, you see; what they meant was that she didn't try, you see. It was getting late and night, and they got mad at her and left her. You couldn't hardly blame them; it was 50 or 60 below, and you couldn't blame them for leaving her. They had to leave her, you know.

"So they came into camp, where we was making camp, where the hunters was supposed to meet us. They came into camp, and they didn't have her with them, and I asked about that. Well, I give them a talkin' to, but that was no good. And I said, 'By God, there has got to be something done.' And I headed back there, do you see, and there she was. That was Dan's wife at Ross River, Mckinnon's boy.

"So, by God, there they were and left that woman alone. Well, the only thing was to see what I could do for her, you see. Well, what did I know? What could I do? There is where it come in, do you see.

"But on Frances Lake, I picked up a doctor book, and that doctor book was telling about all kinds of diseases, you know, but one particular chapter was midwifery, you see, and I started that. Now in midwifery, the only thing that I understood was a sitz bath, you see. That's the only thing, nothin' else. Well, when this woman was in trouble, you see, havin' her kid, the only thing I knowed to do was a sitz bath.

"Well, all I had to give her a sitz bath with was a tea billy, you know, a little small can for makin' tea, and a little small fryin' pan. Now think of that—that's what I had.

"Well, we got back there, cleaned up and sort of got the tent up, and the way I worked that sitz bath was—I had two big towels, you see, put one under her and up over her, and heat that water and poured it down on the towels. By God, it saved her life. Yes sir, she come out of that, she lived. You get into the darndest jackpots when you're out with the Indians, you know. Oh, poor people, oh mercy, mercy, so gentle and so kind and so good.

"When I think of these damned missionaries—Do you know that if these missionaries was in the South they would lynch them. They would never get to a courtroom because they would be lynched, you see."

"They must think about as much of missionaries in the South as they do of revenuers."

"I must tell you one more story about the little kid in the hills back home. A revenuer came into the yard one day when there was nobody there but the kid.

"'Where's your dad, son?' he says to the kid.

"'Down the holler', the kid says, 'he's working at the still.'

"The revenuer says, 'Will you take me there? I'll pay you a dollar.'

"O.K." says the kid, "Give me the dollar."

"'I'll give you the dollar when we get back,' the man says.

"And the kid says 'I'll take the dollar now mister, because you ain't comin' back.'"

We talked of the time he and Steel were up on the Pelly. Let him tell it:

"George Steel was from Missouri and he and I were trapping up towards the headwaters of the Pelly. We had loaded our stuff on a boat, and, with the dogs running along the bank, we poled some 40 miles up the Pelly to a place known as High Bank, and there we established our main camp for the winter. It was pretty late in the fall, and we were getting ready. We had to scout out and blaze some trapline trails, fix up a toboggan, and, oh, there was plenty to do.

"The time he was shot, we had crossed over the Pelly from our main camp and followed an old trail up Willow Creek to an old cabin that would be good for a winter camp. The fellows had been out of it for a couple of years, but it was in good shape.

"We got up in the morning, and it had snowed; there was snow on the brush, so we didn't want to travel. So we said we wouldn't lose a day, we would go out and cut down—there was lots of birch there—and cut down a birch and start to make a toboggan, you see. And so we laid up that day and stayed home. We went out there, and a chicken flew up, and I run back to the cabin to get the .22. And as I was comin' out, I loaded it; but the chicken flew away, and we didn't get it.

"Well, we worked on the toboggan, and then we came in and spent the night. the next mornin', the snow had dropped off the brush, and it was good for travellin'. We was gettin' ready. I was outside puttin' stuff in a dog pack, and I heard a...I was sure it was a shot, in the cabin there. I stepped in, and I said, 'George, didn't I hear a gunshot in here?'

"He said 'yes', he says, look at that', he says, and he was shot through the wrist, right through here. So I took a hold of his hand and looked at it.

"'George', I said, 'you better tie that up and get it taken care of, it's goin' to give you trouble for some time,' I said, 'but it don't amount to anything.'

"'Dawed blast—that—that don't amount to anything. I'm shot down here!' he says.

"My God, when he said that, that scared me. I just unbottoned his pants down, and here the blood had run down from a bullet hole about that far, you see. It wasn't blood at all. When I looked at it, why I seen, my God that wasn't blood, and so I knowed then what was wrong—he was shot through the guts!

"Anyway, I looked at it, and he just—he moved away from me, and I looked at him and his eyes were a workin' just as fast as they could, and he started to fall, and I got him and laid him on the bed.

"Then he started throwin' up. Talk about a sick man! My God, my God! I held his head and done everything—imagine a man alone there with a man in that shape, a man he'd never had a word with. No, sir, if we had a quarrel and I felt like killin' him, why it wouldn't have amounted to do much. No, sir, he was the greatest friend I'd ever had, you know, the greatest man, just a pure damn old farm boy you know, and my God, I couldn't do a thing for him! So studyin' what can I do, I must have went crazy, I don't know anything else—studyin'— what can I do now?

"When I was a kid and us kids at home we used to say, just for fun, if you don't know what to do, pray; and that's what hit me. Yes, sir, it come to me at once. Well, I just walked over there and dropped down on my knees and prayed and prayed in a good loud voice. You could hear me prayin', I didn't whisper that prayer either, I told God, I said, 'God, I'm askin' you this time if you'll only help me and get me out of this jackpot,' I said, 'I'll never ask you for another favour,' I said. Well, imagine, well, no, sir. I didn't intend to ask Him neither. I wasn't fixin' to bother Him. He's bothered enough with these renegades anyway, you know.

"Well, after a spell of prayin' there, I felt easier. I got up perfectly quiet, my nerve was settled, and so I made—I just instantly made up my mind what to do. Go and get help and get him out of that, you see, that was all. I went to Steel, and

I said, 'George', I said, 'I'm goin' to leave you,' I said. 'There's no use of me to stay with you and watch you die.'

"No, I can die just as easy alone as if there was a hundred men with me,' he says, 'I don't mind dyin',' he says.

"So I says, 'George, that's jake,' I says and so, but he says, 'You better get made a paper or somethin', some way,' he says. We didn't have any diaries with us. 'Some way,' he says, 'that I can leave a statement,' he says, 'looked like we'd been fightin',' he says, 'and there should be some statement.'

"Well, I got to lookin' around. I looked at the table. I remember there was an empty butter can and some other trash on the table, and there was a piece of paper. I went and looked at that paper, and I found a part that was clean and nice, and so there was just what I wanted.

"I took that paper, and I took a .22 shell and sharpened the end a bit, and I handed it to him and he wrote, 'shot accidently,' and then he signed his name, and of course that was good enough.

"Then I got him wood, and he would be all right, and put candles and everything close to him, and pulled out. It was 20 miles to Mason's cabin. That was my idea, to go and get Mason and get help, do you see. So I went to Mason's cabin, and of course Mason wasn't there. I wrote on the door with charcoal and turned back. The dogs were follerin' me, and 10 miles back was another old trapper's cabin with an old sleigh in it. As I say, the dogs were follerin' me, they often did that when they weren't tied up. They were trailin' along, so when I got to this old cabin, I wrestled around and with bits of string and rope tied them up to this old sleigh.

"By this time, it was gettin' dark enough so that I couldn't see the trail. Mostly the only thing that I had to follow was the blaze marks on the trees. Lucky the dogs were along. When I got them tied to this old sleigh I just held on to the handles, and the dogs took me back to the cabin.

"When we got back, I turned the dogs loose and didn't make no noise. I knowed where there was a pole that was cut that I was goin' to bring in for wood, but didn't bring it in. I thought I would go out and get that pole and bring it in and get plenty of wood, and go in and take him out and throw him on the sleigh and spend the night there. The next mornin' I would put him in the cabin and fasten it up—that was my idea, you see. I was sure that he was dead.

"But he wasn't dead! Not by a whole lot, you know. Anyway, I threwed that pole down off my shoulder, and turned around and was just goin' to get a candle and get some light in the—you can't see to chop—you can't chop in the dark, you know. I was goin' to light the candle and set it in the door so that it wouldn't blow out and do my choppin', and was just goin' to walk in—

"Dawed blast it! Are you back already?" he says.

"No man ever heard music like that—no man would believe to hear a voice like that.

"Don't you know,' he says 'you have been gone nine hours and a half."

"There I had made what we'd call 40 miles now, in nine and a half hours. That's goin' some. Well, I went in; then he was tellin' me of his fears, you see. He told me that after I had left that no man ever suffered like he did, 'Oh', he said, 'sakes', he said, 'it was awful!' he said. He said he believed that God could do one thing or the other, and he could do it then. He told God, he says 'Kill me or cure me,' he says, 'It's up to you,' he says, 'It makes no difference to me,' he says.

"That instant every bit of pain left him. Now, he didn't lie. I don't believe he lied, no sir. Now wasn't that the greatest faith that you ever heard tell of a man havin'? 'Kill me or cure me, one way or another' he says.

"He was tellin' me he figured the bullet grazed through and come up here and worked out in a hollow place here. He said it was headed straight for his heart if it had went on, he said, before it turned there.

"Oh, my! Poor George! He only had one eye, you know. the doctors in those days didn't understand treatin' cataract, do you see, and they went out monkeyin' with this eye and scattered that, you know, and ruined the one eye altogether. His mother wouldn't even let him go to school, wouldn't let him touch a book. She said she would rather have an ignorant boy than a blind boy. And they were wealthy, you know. They had a big farm in Missouri there and everything, but you know he could hardly read his own writin' when he was with me.

Yukon River "throwing ice" at Fort Selkirk. This was very dangerous—if the ice jammed there was no way off the river. Water travel in these conditions was only done for very urgent reasons.

"It was kind of amusin' to see. He told me one time, them Missourians don't talk about what they have or what they haven't, you see. So you don't know what kind of people are there. And he says, 'Lots of people don't know it, but my old dad has two of as good farms as there are in old Misoo,' he says. Missouri, he meant, 'And $20,000 in the bank.' I thought that was pretty good you know, yes, sir."

"Well, how did you get him out now?"

"Oh, my gosh. I haven't told you about that—oh, my.

"George was fixin' to eat that night, but I figured he oughtn't to do that, and I wouldn't let him. Next morning, I gave him a little canned milk. We hadn't put nothin' on the wound, and it had gotten a little red around the bullet hole during the night. We had nothin' in the way of medicines with us, but I had put on a poultice of soft spruce tree pitch. That kept the wound from healing over and at the same time it drew out the poison.

"I got a rope that we had lashin' our stuff up and put that around the dogs' necks—an old bitch and three pups. When there was no snow, we just used the dogs for packin' and had no sleigh harness for them there. So I rigged up a harness and put him in the sleigh. It was a home-made sleigh, but it was good. It had no nails, but was lashed up with rawhide, and we started out.

"The river had been throwin' ice, had jammed and was raisin' cain one way or another; but we were having a warm spell, and it was running again. There was no snow left of what had fallen, and it took us three days to get 30 miles down river—me and the dogs pullin' and shovin' the sleigh over bare ground. Here was a cabin where we spent the night, and the next day we took this fellow's boat and got into it and started down the river.

"It was colder now and frosty, and fog on the river and ice running with us as we went. We travelled most of the day with me rowin' when I could, but the ice was a kind of a nuisance hitting the oars. Nobody that didn't have to would ever be caught travellin' on a river in these kind of conditions.

"Anyway, along toward the end of the day, the pullin' got harder, do you see. I thought it felt muddy. I had taken my coat off, you see, and I knowed I was going to have to pull hard to get on through, do you see. I had taken my coat off and, uh—so I was diggin' into it, and pretty soon there was something wrong with my oars, they didn't work there when I tried to pull back, you know.

"I couldn't imagine, and so anyway the fog lifted just a little, and I looked under there at the shore, and there we were standin' still in an ice jam. We were standin' still here, and if you can't see the shore, you don't know it even if you are rowin', you see.

"So I went to Steel, and he was lyin' there. I said 'George', I said, 'I figured you would die alone,' I said, 'but I'm dyin' with you,' I said. I figured there was no use makin' any kick that I was goin' right there, because if that ice ever started it would grind that boat up in no time, you know.

"Anyway, he looks out, 'Oh, I don't think there's any danger,' he says, and he laid down again and turned over. Well, this kind of made me sore, you see, to see the nerve of that fellow, without being well and me in health, you know. I went and got to punchin' 'round the side of the boat with a pole and monkeyin' 'round the boat, and he looks out and says, 'You'd better come and get under the blanket with me, you'll get cold up there,' he says.

"So, I come back, and I says, 'Steel, if you can die that damned easy, I'll just show you I can die just as easy,' I wasn't dyin' easy not by a whole lot, no, sir. I liked life too well but I went under the blanket with him and laid there awhile, and there was nothing for me to do, so I got out, and punchin' around the pole would go right down through—there was lots of ice but you couldn't walk on it. It would turn over, you know, so that was out of the question.

"Just then a thought struck me—if I had a big pair of snowshoes, I could go ashore now. Just the thing that was goin' to take me to shore now. My mind run on to that just exactly where it should, do you see. Well, if I had a pair of snowshoes—why not make a pair? Well, how you goin' to make it? Studied a minute. I'll tell you how I'll do that, I'll take a board off the side of the boat, and then I'll have it.

"Well, I took a board off the side of the boat—30-foot boat, you know. I took a board off and put it down—and it was thin, it buckled right up when I got on it. That wouldn't work. I cut that in two and doubled it and laid it out there, and I could get right on that and stand. Now I was as good as gold; all I had to do was take a board off the other side and go right to shore. Anyway, I got to shore. I climbed up on the bank there and cut timber and throwed it down and started—and it was dark when I got him bridged now. No, nothin' to eat, hungry and weak; but I got the bridge into the boat, and I says, 'George, I got a bridge for you, but would be afraid to pack you. I'm all in,' I says.

" 'If you've got a bridge, sure I'll get to shore,' he says.

"I says, 'Do her then,' I says, 'go to it,' I says. So I started gatherin' and gettin' the stuff together, and he started crawlin', and by the time I got the stuff together and got to the shore, he was there, too, crawlin'. And then this bank, you know—and all the rocks, you know, on the shore—the idea of goin' up there and cuttin' brush and wood, and campin' there on them frosty rocks—goodness alive. I knowed enough about campin' that that was a great hardship, you know.

"I said, 'George, I just hate to tackle that, but it's got to be done. I'll go up there and cut brush and stuff and fix a night camp here on the rocks.

" 'Dawed blast it, we won't make camp on no rocks here,' he says.

"I says, 'What will we do?'

" 'We'll go up there,' he says.

"'And you can't walk,' I says, 'what are you talkin' to me about that.'
"'I'll show you, come here,' he says, 'and get down on your hands and knees,' he says.

"I went over there and got down on my hands and knees; he put his arm right across my neck here, and we started out and went right up the bank—nothin' to it at all. Didn't take me long then to fix up a good camp, and we put in the night there.

"I went on down river the next morning and ran into two Frenchmen and a Lord Talmish, an English lord, and so I went in. "Where did you come from so early in the morning?" they asked. They were strangers to me, that's the first time I had seen them. They were about eight miles from where I had left Steel. So I told them my partner was shot up the river there, and I said, 'I've got to get him out.'

"The Englishman says, 'I don't see how in the world you'll do it,' he says, 'the river is not fit to travel on,' he says, 'and it's all brushy,' he says. 'You can't get through the brush', he says, 'I don't know how in the world you'll get him out', he says.

"And the two Frenchmen spoke up and said the same thing. I knowed right then that this is their first trip into the bush, you see. They were all right, but didn't know anything. So anyway I said, 'Braden is livin' two miles below,' I said, 'I'll go down and see him.'

"So I went down to Braden's, and when I went in, he said, 'Where's Steel?' And so I told him about Steel, you know. So he turned around, and he says, 'Donna get us somethin' to eat', he says, 'we'll go up there and bring him down here', he says. Now that sounded pretty good you know.

"So we got his dogs—he had some no-account dogs—so we got them ready and took off. When we were passin' the two Frenchmen and the English lord, this Lord Talmish, why one of the Frenchmen went with us with their team. Oh, they had a big dog team. So we went up, and we camped; and the next day we got him down to Braden's, and it took 12 days at Braden's place till the river set, and then we hauled him to Selkirk and sent him to Dawson on the winter stage.

"It was 24 days before he reached the doctor and 26 days before he was operated on, and still that man lived, you know."

"He certainly must have been pretty tough. Where would he likely be now?"

"The next season, we travelled to the head waters of the Pelly River and done our trappin' around Frances Lake. Come spring, George went back to Missouri; he married a home town girl, then went cattle ranchin' in Idaho, and they raised a family. So far as I know, he is still living. He was a fine man!"

Heading For
The Nahanni

Fred Guder

Heading for the Nahanni

Fred Guder as a young man with a moose calf at Carmacks.

Fred Guder is now seventy-eight years of age, still active and hearty, and still heads for the hills every spring to spend some time in one or another of his cabins Guder is like a good many men who have spent their days in the wilderness of the north, he likes to keep going. He wants to keep the abundant good health he has always enjoyed, which has been due largely to the simple and rigourous life he has led.

As we sit talking about his younger days it is impossible not to be impressed by the unbelieveable differences between then and now. Fifty years ago there was a vast difference between the amount of time, effort, and labour it required to travel in the north from one place to another. First there was the difficulty of always having to carry everything needed. To some extent a supply of food— flour, tea, salt, sugar, etc.,—food that could not be acquired from hunting. Then there was a tent, a small stove, and a suitable supply of clothes and blankets.

Each man had his dogs—work dogs. In the summer when on the move, the dogs carried packs or rode on the raft or in the boat, or ran along the bank. In the winter they pulled the toboggans; but summer or winter they had to be fed, and they lived on either fish or meat. Such a thing as dog food that could be purchased by the sack had not been heard of in those days.

Today if Guder wants to go from Whitehorse to Dawson, some three hundred odd miles to the north, it will take him from five to six hours by car, or an hour and a half by air.

He told me in some detail of a trek he made over into the Nahanni Valley when he was a young man. A trek that took him from August until spring. During the winter he came out once by dog team to pick up some of the supplies he had cached, and then went back to finish the winter trapping.

This trip began by boat from Ross River on the Pelly and Guder considered it more of an adventure than anything else. Some Indians had found gold on the Nahanni side, which had created an interest in the area. Some men had already been over to investigate the rumours of the finding of gold in quantities. Bill Atkinson, Poole Field and Ole Bradvick were among them.

His boat was a sixteen foot canoe, and to find out how much stuff he was going to be able to take he tried his canoe out in the river loaded down with rocks. When he had the load just right he weighed the rocks, and discovered he was going to be able to take nine hundred pounds.

To carry his canoe upstream against the current required the use of a pole rather than paddles; so he fitted a good dry stick with an iron point. At places where it was possible for him to go along the bank he pulled his canoe with a rope attached a little back from the front, so that the effect of pulling it forward also kept it out in the stream. When the going was good he was able to cover twenty miles in a single day, but this was certainly the exception rather than the rule. There were two hundred and fifty miles to cover on the Pelly River before he would be forced to lay up his boat, due in part to the onset of hundred and fifty miles from his point of departure.

Following him along on the bank were his dogs—seven of them—that had to be fed with meat or fish once a day. Later they would be indispensable to him, but in the meantime they still had to be fed, and it required a considerable amount of time and effort to hunt for these dogs. Game was abundant, fortunately, and he was a good shot. To augment the supply of meat he also carried with him a long light pole some twenty feet in length, and fitted at the end with a detachable hook, made from a file, to which was fastened a line. In the fall all the rivers on the Yukon watershed abound with a big red-coloured salmon that comes in from the ocean to spawn. A good-sized salmon weighs up to forty pounds, makes excellent dog food and food for himself as well, and he had learned from the Indians how to make and use the long pole for spearing these fish.

The dogs were able to hunt a little for themselves, but frequently became distracted by something and took off. The first time this happened, he went on two or three miles upstream and when they did not show up he waited. Eventually he had to go back, and there they were on the beach where he had last seen them.

The dogs did not seem to be able to reason. The fact that they had been travelling upstream for many days would have made it obvious to a reasoning creature that he had continued on upstream. Not so with the dogs. When they came back to the river and he was gone, their reasoning powers did not take over. They required him to be in sight or to have left a scented trail along the bank that they could follow. On another occasion they took out after a pack of young wolves, and when they finally came back to where he was waiting some of them had been badly bitten.

Sometimes it was the other way round. He had killed a moose some distance from the river and was going back the following day with the dogs to bring in the meat. The dogs ran on ahead when he approached the place where the moose had been shot, and when he arrived on the scene they had a good sized black bear, that had been feeding on the meat, torn to shreds.

Two of the seven dogs he had, belonged to Pete Boxon, a Norwegian trapper who lived on the second of the three Pelly Lakes, and it was his intention to return these dogs on his way by. When he arrived at Wolf Canyon he knew it would be about a twenty mile walk across country to the lake where his friend, Pete, had his main cabin.

Day after day he alternately toiled on the river, or hunted in order to keep the dogs fed; and soon the river became more and more shallow and less in width, and the air grew colder and the days shorter as the fall advanced. Then he got out his woollen mitts, because the water was freezing on the pole with which he pushed his canoe. He found too that, as he poled along in the very shallow water, the front end of his canoe seemed to want to pull down, and it was then that he must jump in and pull the canoe through to deep water again. He ended up wet every day, but he used to put off getting wet as long as he was able, and some days were better than others.

Toward the end of the day he selected a good place to camp while it was still light, and as soon as he had a good fire going and was able to dry out, roast some moose ribs, make some bannock and some tea with plenty of sugar, then he could take it easy by the fire and enjoy smoking his pipe.

Several times he met with Indians on the river, and when he told them where he was going they said this was no good! There were several bands of Indians in the valley who did not like white men, and they would probably shoot him. He told them he was able to shoot as well. He had heard, nevertheless, of instances where white men had not returned from travelling in the area. As it happened, he lived with one of these bands of Indians for several months, travelled and hunted with them.

Fred Guder drying cariboo meat at Ross River.

On one occasion, while he was resting for a moment during the day, an old Indian on a small raft was coming by and stopped. They made a fire and a billy can of tea, and smoked and talked and visited for awhile. During the conversation he was able to learn many things about the area to which he was journeying, and also something of the Indian philosophy.

On another occasion he joined an Indian who was paddling up to a small lake, where they put in a fish net. The lake was a good feeding ground for ducks and geese, and being the fall of the year it was, naturally, the time the migratory birds were headed south. But, although the birds were on the lake in considerable numbers, the two men were unable to get close enough with the boat to get a shot with the single barrelled shot gun Guder had along. Accordingly, they waited until it was dark and then, with his companion paddling quietly and Guder in the front of the boat with his gun, they put out onto the lake again and moved carefully over to where the quacking was the loudest. When he figured he was close enough, he fired a shot in the direction of the noise and was lucky enough to bag three Mallards. Subsequently they were signalled to the shore with lights and picked up two other Indians to journey back to the Pelly where they were camped. When these men, who had heard the shooting in the dark, saw the three ducks they told Guder that he must have eyes like a lynx. Guder was content to have established such a reputation as he travelled into what might turn out to be hostile country.

Soon after that, he was overtaken by a fairly large party of Indians, travelling upstream as he was, so he travelled with them until they arrived at Wolf Canyon, when they stopped to rest and hunt and get ready for a three mile portage around the canyon. The party consisted of five or six men, several women, a couple of youths and some children. They also had something in the neighbourhood of fifty dogs.

He observed that the women do the work around the camp and on the trail, and the men provide the meat for food and the skins for clothing as a result of their hunting. The food consisted mainly of meat, and in those days the Indians purchased very little in the way of groceries because they were not used to them. Guder himself had only the barest essentials. He could not get butter when he left, so he made some of a sort for himself. He cooked caribou bones, and then mixed the jelly with a portion of fat and some salt and sugar. When he had used the candles he brought with him, he used bear and caribou fat with a wick for light in his tent. Such oil does not provide the best light, and he found he needed to keep it close to the stove so it would stay in a liquid state.

His tent he seldom bothered to set up unless he planned to stay in one place for awhile, or when it was raining or snowing. Mostly he had an open camp and did his cooking over an open fire. When he did use the tent, he had a small tin stove for heat and for cooking. Later, when he was staying in the valley, the

Indians offered him a marten pelt worth $135.00 for this little stove, but he was not foolish enough to part with it.

Soon they had to apply themselves to getting their boats and gear transported along the three mile portage to the river above the canyon. The Indians, who had three boats, made an attempt to haul the largest one up through the canyon with ropes on either side, but it turned out to be a poor idea and the boat was damaged before the effort was abandoned. It was fortuitous for Guder, because in return for his fixing up the boat, they gave him a hand to get his stuff and his canoe, which weighed two hundred pounds, moved to the upper river. Here he made himself a fairly good camp, and securing his provisions against the depredations of bears and wolverines, he took the two dogs that belonged to his friend Pete Boxon, and set off across country to the middle one of the three Pelly Lakes.

He covered the twenty miles during the course of one day, but the excursion was a miserable one because of the rain. The route was hilly, with thick brush, and here and there an open space where the going was good. The rest of the time he was able to follow game trails, if they happened to be heading in the direction he required, and when this was not the case he became wetter than ever through his contact with the thick brush.

All through the north are trails, some made and used for centuries by the Indians, whose passages back and forth to hunting, fishing and trapping areas has kept them well used and open. Other trails are made by the passage of wild animals in their wanderings, and they of course, head off in many directions. Even the well established trails that are used by man are also used by animals, and if a tree should happen to fall across the path an animal will not step over or go around it, but will start a new trail that leads nowhere in particular.

Guder did not require a compass. He had learned by experience and from the Indians how to keep going in the right direction. In an area where there are hills and mountains for landmarks, and rivers, streams and valleys to follow, he experienced no difficulty in finding the way. Apart from this he had become impervious to the discomforts he experienced practically every day—cold, wet, fatigue—his mind was schooled to accept these things as part of every day living.

His arrival late in the evening was a delight to his friend Pete Boxon. Pete was already twenty years in the Yukon, first as a gold miner during the rush at the turn of the century, and then as a trapper. Once every year he made a hundred and fifty mile trip by boat to the store and trading post at Ross River to sell his furs and replenish his supplies for the ensuing year. He had always impressed Guder with his learning, and it was said of him that he had been a professor before coming to the Yukon in quest of gold. He also had the reputation of being a good shot, a nice gentlemanly accomplishment. He made the best part of his living hunting and trapping wolves on the three lakes where he lived both summer and winter. In the summer he grew a good garden, and the younger man, who had been encouraged to stay over for a day, had the two dogs which he returned loaded down with turnips for his return journey.

He hunted for his dogs and rested for several days following his return from the Pelly Lakes, and then loaded up his canoe and continued his travels up river. His Indian friends travelled in the same direction, and they were able to assist each other on the several places that were hard to pass. The river abounded with rapids and rough spots as they ascended into higher ground, and Guder was wondering how his return trip would go next spring at a time of high water. After several days of this torturous travel they arrived at the mouth of a small stream, and here he left his Indian friends because it was too difficult for them to travel on the small stream, and they also wished to camp for awhile and hunt.

One of Guder's cabins—the window, a sugar sack dipped in wax.

They had their first snow. Guder elected, however, to continue on up the river; but the travel, as well as being difficult, was decidedly unpleasant. The pole was continually iced up, and many times he found it necessary to jump into the water and pull through the very shallow places. He did, however continue on for several more days, and when the river became just too shallow and started to run with ice, then he pitched his tent. He was roughly one hundred and fifty miles from his point of departure.

Two days later he returned late in the evening from a fruitless hunt on the

Lake LaBarge, 1920. Hand-made boats cost about $1 a foot.

mountain, and found the river completely covered over with ice. Not only was the river frozen but, due to a blockage caused by ice farther down, the level of the surface had risen several feet and there was his canoe made fast to what used to be the shore, about thirty feet out. It was necessary to wade out, breaking the thin ice as he went, untie the canoe and bring it safely up on the opposite shore and into his camp before it froze in solid.

He had no wood cut for a fire, so he was compelled to go out in the dark with his axe in order to get some. This was the time he cut his knee, for he found it difficult to cut wood properly in the dark, even after he was able to find some that was suitable for his purpose. A bad cut or two, and a man who spends his time alone in the bush soon learns that it pays to be careful with his axe or hunting knife. When limbing trees he steps over and cuts off the limbs and knots on the opposite side of the log to which he is standing. On this occasion he was cold, wet, and in a hurry, and it was getting dark. The axe glanced off a hard knot and opened his knee beside the kneecap.

Meat supply was soon at an end, but he was not able to get about well enough to hunt, so his dogs went hungry. Not far from his camp was a beaver house, and although he tried to catch some of the beaver with steel traps, he had no luck with it. Otherwise he busied himself as best he could preparing to build a cache, because now he was to leave his boat and a good part of his provisions until he returned in the spring.

Soon he would have a good sized portion of cross beams and poles set between three or four trees about eight feet above the ground. On the platform he would pile his stuff and cover it with a good canvas. A permanent cache to be used year in and year out would be just like a small cabin, roof and all, but set high off the ground on trees. It was the custom to nail a couple of lengths of stove pipe or some kind of tin on the trees leading up to the cache to inhibit the climbing animals from gaining access to the food and chewing up the rest of the stuff.

Guder knew that he did not have to concern himself about thievery by anything but animals. In the vast, sparsely or completely unpopulated areas of the north it is the unwritten law that caches are left alone; and it does not go well with a man who gets caught molesting another man's cache. Should it happen that some circumstance causes him to be in dire need of provisions, then he is certainly free to make use of them as far as his need goes. His first concern thereafter is to put the cache back to its original state or see that the owner has been advised and payment is made in part if not in kind.

When his knee healed to the point where he could move more freely, then his first need was to hunt meat for his dogs. While he was hunting he came across the fresh tracks of a band of Indians. He followed them up, and came upon the camp of some of the Indians he had left on the river below the gorge, and they provided him with a packsack of meat to carry back for his dogs. He spent a couple of days more, when he got back to camp, before he hit the trail again. He finished building the cache and sorted out what he was going to take and what he must, of necessity, leave behind. He made up a pack for each dog, and each was required to carry something in the neighbourhood of forty pounds.

When he reached the place where the Indians had been, he found they had moved on again, but were soon overtaken at a point where they had stopped to trap and hunt as was their want. These Indians were going to travel in the vicinity of the Nahanni, the same as he, so they decided to travel together. Most of the men were away hunting, and when he had taken care of his dogs he decided he had better hunt as well. Accordingly, he prepared to set out.

The old chief asked him in which direction he intended to go, and when he told the old man, he was advised against it, and it was suggested that he take off in a different direction. Guder did not know, and the old man did not tell him, why he did not want him to go in the direction in which he was determined to go. Later he learned that the Indians had already been hunting in that direction, and had come across the track of a huge bear. The old man was afraid Guder might run into this bear, and get hurt or be killed.

Regardless of the old chief's advice, Guder set out, and sure enough he found the bear. He was snowshoeing along in about six inches of snow, his breath coming out in clouds of white vapour, and the only sound in the woods that he was aware of was the rythmic crunch and drag of his snowshoes. Along the side of a dry creek bed he came upon the huge tracks, and followed them. He knew the bears would be holing up about this time. What he did not know was that the Indians had killed a couple of moose and cached the meat under the snow and put brush over it, and the bear had found this meat.

He came to a place in a hollow where the Indian hunters had made a fire to boil some water for tea, and he noted the bear had rolled in the ashes; and then, of a sudden, he seemed to become aware of another presence in the woods there with him. He put the hood of his parka back to uncover his ears and he stood still to watch and listen, and then he moved forward again and stopped. Then, through his clouded breath he saw the bear ahead. It made a couple of jumps and disappeared from view.

At the sight of the bear the whole woods came alive, instead of appearing empty and still. His senses sharpened, and all the power of his body seemed to concentrate itself in his eyes and ears. He stood stock still again, but could hear no sound nor could he see any movement. The bear had not run, he would have seen him if he had. There was open country beyond, so he knew it had stayed near somewhere.

Carefully, very carefully, he put an extra shell in his rifle, slipped out of his snowshoes and his pack, and closed in moving along very slowly. It was at the cache of meat that Guder saw the bear crouched down behind the pile. All he could see was the top of the head, and the small eyes looking at him over the brush.

If Guder had not been able initially, to sense the presence of the bear, he would not have been alive to tell the story. Had he been snowshoeing along in a normal manner and gone on by, intent on the bear's tracks, his parka hood effectively shielding his eyes and ears from sights and sounds to the side and rear, he would have been subjected to a charge accompanied by a terrifying roar the very moment he faced away from the bear. If he had walked boldly up in the direction of the brush pile, the bear would have seen fit to defend the cache of meat in no uncertain a manner, and that would also have brought down the curtain and ended the story then and there.

The very fact that he was actually stalking the bear precluded a surprise attack from it. No animal, without serious provocation, will make a frontal attack on something sneaking up on it. The bear's whole existence depends upon its ability to stalk effectively. It was obviously, therefore, well aware of the fact that it was being stalked, and it must have felt also, that there was imminent danger inherent in the creature that would dare to stalk him—the lord of the woods. Therefore, it remained crouched behind the brush pile on the meat it claimed for its own, and waited, it would seem, a little perplexed.

Guder knew there was no point in shooting the bear between the eyes in the classical manner, more particularly with its head stretched out toward him, because he knew a bear has a very thick skull and a small brain cavity, and a bullet striking on a slant will travel around beneath the scalp instead of penetrating to the brain where it will do most good. He raised his rifle slowly, aimed at the tip of the bear's nose, squeezed the trigger, and that is where the bullet struck. The rifle, a 30-40 Winehester, was firing a 220 grain bullet, the impact of which caused the bear's head to heave back as it reared up. His second shot hit the bear in the neck, and the third, it transpired, penetrated the skull beside the ear and, with that, it dropped behind the brush out of sight. Guder quit shooting and waited. With consummate care he put three more shells in his rifle, and then carefully picked his way around behind the brush pile. There lay the bear in a still heap, and after poking the body with the barrel of his rifle, Guder stood amazed at the size of the animal he had killed.

The bear was so big and heavy he could not roll it over onto its back to skin it out. Eventually he scooped out the snow away from one side, and he was able then to roll the limp mass into the depression. Opening up the hide, Guder found the old bear extremely fat. He found a layer of fat along its back under the hide three inches thick, and he knew the bear was ready to hibernate and most probably would have denned up during the next heavy snow fall.

He removed the head and, fixing it to his pack, carried it back to the Indian camp where to his surprise, it caused considerable excitement and a great deal of rejoicing. A large grizzly bear is particularly dangerous, and they have at times been known to come right into an Indian camp. They fear nothing, not even fire.

When an Indian encounters such a bear while hunting, he will get out of the way if it is at all possible. Never would he attempt to kill a grizzly unless he had a distinct advantage of some kind, or there are several hunters together.

All the Indians in camp gathered to see his trophy, and again Guder was well pleased and felt lucky to be establishing himself as a hunter and as an asset, rather than a liability to the Indians with whom he was to spend some considerable time.

The following day, with some of the younger Indians still in camp, and some pack dogs, he returned and brought back the moose meat, some of the bear meat, and the fat and the huge hide, which was more weight than he would have cared to carry for any distance. Because his tent was still at the cache and he was using an open camp where the Indians were, he folded the flesh side of the hide in, laid it out, and used it to sleep on. The men of the band, when they returned from their hunting, were horrified at this; and were quick to prophesy endless misfortune, because they considered the bear was not dead yet—not indeed, until his hide had been dried.

Guder could understand their feelings with regard to this because he knew they were bound to have ideas connected with the supernatural, as all men have. And who was to say that some incident that could be construed as bad luck that took place subsequently would have taken place anyway, or was the direct result of angering the spirit of a bear by sleeping on its green hide. He was certainly not going to let it bother him, in any case.

The next day he carried it down river to his cache, stretched it out to freeze, and put it under the tarp with the rest of his stuff. He packed his tent on one of the dogs, rigging it so that it filled both sides of the pack. In the bottom of the pack he put ammunition, something heavy to keep the weight low, and the small tin stove he tied on the top. On his own back and on the dogs he had everything he needed for the winter. In his cache was a good supply of food and other necessities against the time of his return over the same route.

The Indians had moved on when he arrived back at the camping place, but he overtook them in a day or two, and they all travelled together. They would keep on the move for three or four days, and then perforce, stop and hunt.

On one occasion Guder and his companions shot a couple of moose toward the close of the day, and camped beside the meat. When the dressing and skinning was done, and they had all supped on roast meat and tea, Guder's nose began to bleed copiously and there was no way, it seemed, that he could get it stopped.

Now it was the Indians who had their innings, and they were quick to remind him of the bad luck they prophesied for him because of his sleeping on the green hide of the grizzly bear. Everything he tried was of no avail. He put snow over his face and on the back of his neck, but the steady flow would not stop.

One of the Indians finally said he would fix it for him, and by this time of course Guder was willing to try any expedient at all. He was told to put a piece of meat on a stick, lay down and stick it in the snow close to his head. This he did, and when the bleeding stopped it was the cause of much happiness on the part of everybody.

And so they continued on their way toward the valley. If they passed through an area where the fur was plentiful they stayed longer, put out steel traps and built deadfalls for marten. One of the Indians shot a marten out of a tree where he had chased it, and provided himself with a pelt worth $125—a great deal of money in those days.

The land was full of game for meat and good fur for trade at the outposts, and it was no trouble at all for a small band such as Guder travelled with to be able to support itself adequately.

Then it came time to make toboggans so the dogs could pull the loads over the snow instead of carrying them in packs. For this purpose they required the tough wood from the birch tree, but they made use of spruce when there was no birch in the area, as was the case in this instance. The spruce toboggans would not stand rough treatment, but they would do until an area was reached where birch could be obtained. Guder paid one of the older men to make him a good toboggan and a pair of six-foot snowshoes. The snow was getting deeper now, and while the smaller snowshoes he had were good enough for the trail he needed the longer ones for hunting in the deep snow.

He found his life with the Indians interesting, and he realized they lived in a far different environment than he had come from; and as a consequence of this had a set of values far removed from the values held by himself. Naturally, their philosophy and outlook were vastly different as well, but certainly not unsuited to the conditions in which they found themselves.

At first he was taken aback, but gradually his understanding became more lucid and he found himself more readily led to reconcile their behaviour.

As they made their way down into the valley itself, one of the young men became ill. He ate nothing for a space of five days. Guder noticed that one of the men had a bottle of medicine of some description, and asked why it was he did not give some of it to the boy.

"Sometime my woman get sick too", he was told; and that was the end of that. The medicine, probably cascara or some sort of laxative, may or may not have been of any help to the unfortunate young man, and certainly no one can ever tell what was the cause of his death. His step-father sat in the tent smoking his pipe, and when the boy died they simply pulled the tent off from over him and covered the body with brush.

Later, one of the women gave birth to a still-born child. They simply hung the little body in a tree and moved on.

It was while they were busy manufacturing toboggans and snowshoes that Guder set off one day to bring in some moose meat. He took fifteen of the pack dogs and a couple of the Indian boys. His rifle he left in camp, because there was no need to carry it on this occasion. He knew that any self-respecting bear would be denned up by this time, and he figured the moose had been killed off for miles in any direction from the camp. The meat they planned to bring in was in the neighbourhood of six miles from the camp, and when they had covered most of this distance the dogs ran off and cornered a big bull on a hillside.

The area had been burned over and was fairly bare except for the skeleton trees left standing. There were bushes here and there, but because of the bareness of the area most of the snow had blown clear. The dogs were worrying the bull from all sides, and it did not seem disposed to take off; so Guder knew he must kill this moose in order to get the dogs away and accomplish what he had come to do.

All he had with him was an ordinary "Wilson" butcher knife; and so he tied this to the end of a stick ten feet long, told the boys to stay back in the clear out of danger, and started moving in to kill this moose. The dogs were keeping the moose busy. Its ears were laid back and its eyes were rolling and wide, and there was no question in Guder's mind that the animal was getting into a furious mood. Nonetheless, he moved in slowly with his makeshift spear ready. He stood straight up and inched along as unobtrusively as he could. The closer he was able to get the more slowly he moved, until he was within reach and the moose's attention was, for the moment, directed toward the side away from him. Then, with all his strength and as quickly and accurately as he could, he shoved the knife in behind the moose's shoulder.

He must have thought, naturally enough, that if he stuck the knife into the moose's heart it would simply drop down dead. In any event, he certainly was not prepared for the explosion of activity that the moose directed toward him the moment he struck it with the knife. It swung and reared and, slashing with its front feet, made to put Guder out of the fight then and there; and it certainly would have if Guder had not been lucky. He tried to get behind a bit of bush, but slipped and fell to his hands and knees, and was conscious of the moose's front feet all around him and on him. By some means and with the help of the dogs, he got clear and slipped and slithered down the hillside for about twenty or thirty feet. He was fully expecting to have the moose on top of him again, but the dogs had effectively re-engaged its attention. He felt like he had been hit by a freight train, but he was able to get to his feet. He was liberally covered with blood from the moose. His hat had been knocked off and was missing, and one of his rear pockets, that had held a flat tin of tobacco, had been torn off. Nothing was broken, however, so he went back up the slope to where the dogs still had the moose furiously engaged.

He carefully recovered his knife and stick, which were lying on the ground, and circling to the uphill side, he threw it this time like a spear and caught the moose low and back along the underside. He must have inflicted quite a good sized cut, because he could then see a little of the gut protruding from the wound. By this time the moose had already sustained one severe wound and had also received sundry nips and slashes from the dogs, so that the second knife wound did not create the havoc that the first one had. He was able to get his weapon once more, and this time throwing it again from the uphill side landed it in the moose's neck, where it broke off and fell to the ground.

The moose was beginning to flag. Blood was running from the first wound in the same manner as condensed milk from a can. Guder needed his knife again, but it was lying now beneath the embattled moose and there was no hope of getting it. He looked around for something he could use as a weapon, and he spotted the dog pack that contained his axe. It was lying uphill about thirty feet from the scene of activity, and left where the dog evidently wriggled out of it during the melee. He recovered the axe, and now the only thing he could think of doing was to try to fell a tree on the moose so that it would lie down. Oddly enough, during the whole of the encounter up to this time the moose had stayed pretty much in the same place, so Guder selected a tree uphill and within reach, and started chopping on the dry wood. He was half way finished when the moose, battle weary and weak from the loss of blood, lay down of its own accord. Immediately the dogs were on top, and Guder moved in quickly before the dogs should cause the moose to get up again, and hit it with the axe between the horns. This seemed to have no effect at all, so he hit again. The third time he reached a little farther back, and when the corner of the axe penetrated to the moose's brain its suffering was ended.

There was little point in going after the other meat at this juncture, when they had fresh meat at hand, so they set about butchering the moose they had just killed. It would be dark shortly, so they did not even take time to boil the billy can for tea. They had been out for the best part of the day, and the boys to allay their hunger cut six inch pieces of the small intestine, and stripping the contents out between their fingers, ate these while they worked.

To anybody else but Guder, this would have appeared to be a strange and repulsive thing to do. Over the period of time he spent with the Indians he had given much thought to the behaviour of these primitive people, and was able the see this as a perfectly sensible and normal thing for them to have done. Certainly these Indian children were not the same as other children he had known. To them, all their lives, the moose had been considered as their main source of food. He reflected they had never tasted candy or cake or even bread, and when he considered these things he was able to reconcile their behaviour and associate it with their way of life.

Finally they were loaded up and set out, it was then Guder found the going a little tough. His hips and back were very sore and he found he must travel more slowly than the two youngsters and the pack dogs. By the time he reached camp the children had been in for some time and related the story of the day's happenings long before he arrived. He went straight to his tent and put on a pot of meat to cook, and was getting himself tidied up a little when a delegation of Indians filed in with long, serious faces.

They explained to Guder that it was a very foolish thing for him to have assailed the moose with only a butcher knife tied to the end of a stick. Guder was somewhat amused at this. He felt their remarks simply reiterated what he had already discovered by personal experience.

Actually, what they were afraid of was the fact that there had been some white men killed over in that country and it was supposed to have been Indians that were responsible. The Hudson Bay factor at Fort Liard had told them if there were any more who got killed in the area the Indians would not be supplied with any more ammunition.

At this, Guder told them if anything happened to him, if he got killed in some way, all they had to do was make a good strong cache and put him in it and then go and get the nearest white man, bring him back to look the body over, and that would put them in the clear. The difficulty with this proposition was they might have had to travel several hundred miles in order to find a white man, in 1918!

As they travelled and hunted and trapped, they eventually reached a point some 150 miles down into the valley from the summit, and here they made a more or less permanent camp. Guder found himself a good cabin that had been built quite a few years before by Del VanGorder and Ira VanBibber when they had sojourned and trapped in the valley in that area; and he fixed it up here and there and made his home camp. He was comfortable for the winter, and he had nothing to do but keep himself and his dogs supplied with meat, and trap as much good fur as he was able, to make the trip pay for itself.

He started out to set deadfalls and steel traps along the rim of a long valley. He took two dogs and their packs, and by the end of the fourth day, in spite of making his trap sets, he had covered quite a piece of country. Also, he had by this time used up everything he had with him in the way of food. He anticipated he would be able to shoot a moose along the way, but had been unable to do so, due likely to the noise his dogs were making with their packs in the low brush. Whenever he spotted a moose he was unable to get close enough for a shot.

On the evening of the fourth day, while he was finishing the last of his cold roast moose, his knife slipped and he received a bad cut on the palm of his left hand. Also, he lost his pipe, which did not really affect him materially but it caused him to sense or feel the possible start of a series of mishaps that would eventually compound themselves to the point where he would find himself unable to cope. He knew by this time that when misfortunes start to double up, then he must stop and seriously consider his position.

He was four days from his cabin, his hand was cut, and he was out of food. The sky had been clear now for several days and it was crisp and cold, and there was no doubt it was getting colder. He decided he would be taking too much of a chance to stay out longer, and the thing to do was to head for his cabin, and travel day and night until he got there. Accordingly, the following morning he set out.

After a few miles he experienced a sense of relief when he came across the track of a porcupine in the snow—a fresh track. He followed it up, but his elation was short lived, for the tracks disappeared into a hole among some large rocks and he was unable to get at it. He tried to smoke it out, but all he accomplished was the loss of an hour or two of time. More and more he began to feel the urgency of his position. At all other times of difficulty he had felt he had control of his situation, and now when he saw himself beginning to loose control, he wondered if he might make a bad decision. He pressed on steadily, and travelled the rest of the day without finding anything he could eat.

On the second day he ate the bait he had left at his trap sets whenever he came to one, and this helped him considerably. When the opportunity afforded, he moved along the streams because there was no bush and it was much better going. He was aware of the danger he was courting in doing this, but he considered that in the circumstances he should push his luck a little in order to gain time and distance.

The Nahanni Valley has numberless hot springs, and in many places merely warm springs that thin the ice out from below, creating a real hazard for any living thing walking over the top. Sometimes there are actually open water holes, and sometimes these are covered by a thin crust of snow. Guder was keeping up a good pace. He was using up the distance between his cabin and himself, trying to pull away from the circumstances that seemed to be overtaking him, and he was keeping to the open space afforded by a creek. He thought he heard something behind him and stopped, put back his parka hood and looked around. He saw nothing behind him, but when he turned to move forward again his eye caught the dark shape in front of him, and he knew it was a hole in the snow over open water.

Gently, on his six-foot snowshoes, he pussy-footed back a little and then over to and up the bank. He knew perfectly well that all he had to do was get wet, at these temperatures, and he was finished. Something had stopped him from getting a dunking at this critical time, and he took some comfort from this fact. Later in the day he shot a ptarmigan, which he didn't bother to cook—but ate raw.

That night he stopped and built a fire, and rested for awhile. His hand was bothering. It had become infected, so he scraped out the wound with his knife and rubbed in some "Minards" liniment, and that seemed to help it some. Early the next day he came across another porcupine track which he followed up, and this one he was able to bag. He cooked and ate the liver, and divided the remainder between his two hungry dogs; and he knew now that with but a short distance still to go he was out of danger, and had control of his situation again.

A man needs to be out by himself for long periods in order to adequately develop that peculiar sense that tells him when he needs to take stock and consider or reconsider what he is doing. He felt he had made the correct decision in this instance, and soon was back in his cabin where he had plenty of dry meat, fat, tea and some sugar. There he was able to soak his infected hand in hot water and clear up the infection before it also got out of control.

He was able to hunt and trap again, and join sometimes with the Indians in these endeavours. Always he must retain their respect, and never under any circumstance show any sign of weakness. He knew they realized he was a man out of his usual environment; and they would turn this to their advantage in any way they could if the opportunity ever presented itself.

He was enjoying the winter in his snug cabin. Game was plentiful, and there was also an abundance of good fur for trapping. He made a good load of dried moose meat, and his cache contained frozen livers, hearts, kidneys, etc. that he knew he must eat as well in order to remain in good health. Together with these delicacies, of course, he saved parts of the fat gut, which when turned inside out and boiled, is fatty and rich in carbohydrates, and excellent to have along while travelling and camping in cold weather.

His lead dog presented him with a batch of five pups, which added a note of domesticity to the scene. At this time the Indians were camped across the river from his cabin and the chief, who had expressed a desire for one of the pups, was told that he certainly might have one when the time came for them to be weaned.

Everything seemed to be going along fine until the chief came for his pup, and selected the one that Guder himself had taken a fancy to and was not about to part with. He told the chief he could have any two of the others in the circumstances, but this particular one he wished to keep for himself. The chief's contention was if he could not have the one he had set his heart on, then he did not want any at all. Guder told him with regard to that, he could suit himself; and it was following this that he began to notice the chief's efforts to turn the rest of the people against him.

He got the cleaning rod stuck in his rifle, and it took him two days of soaking it in grease behind the stove, and whittling moose horn to try to drive it out; and it was while he was working at this the chief and some of the other men came to his cabin. They demanded that he return the toboggan and the snowshoes he had already paid for. These were stashed on the roof of his cabin.

Guder countered with a show of hostility and belligerence that put an end to any antipathy the rest of the Indians may have felt. He carefully wiped the grease from his hands, picked up the detached rifle barrel in a very businesslike manner and, confronting the group, told them that the first man that touched any one thing in his camp was going to be in for a good deal of trouble. He had every intention of using the rifle barrel, if need be, and this fact must have made itself manifest to the Indians, because they immediately backed off and left and that was the end of the matter.

Soon after that Guder began to realize that the Indians were playing a game of freeze-out with him. They knew his groceries had been used up long since and soon he would feel the necessity to journey back to his cache, 150 miles to the summit, to replenish his supplies; and they would have preferred to have him go first and break the trail for them. They knew he would not be satisfied to go for very long on a diet of straight meat. On the other hand, Guder reasoned if the Indians could subsist on straight meat, so could he. He certainly had all the meat he required, both for himself and for his dogs. He had tea yet, and some sugar, and he had learned from the Indians themselves that if he boiled successive dinners of meat in the same water it became so salty it was bitter to the taste. And so he went about his daily business and sat tight; and sooner than he expected the Indians ran low in ammunition. He returned one day from a hunt with one of the Lower Post men, and found them gone. Most of the men and one woman had headed back, and Guder and his companion took the trail behind them as soon as they could get ready to go.

In spite of the fact that the trail was being broken for them, Guder and his companion were experiencing considerably more than normal in the way of privations. The temperature was low, better than minus fifty degrees, and Guder's companion had a bad case of diarrhea, and they had to stop frequently and build a fire so the man's needs could be taken care of without his having to freeze to death. The first night on the trail was possibly the worst, for they camped in a sort of canyon. There was no point in going back to a more suitable camping place, and it was too late in the day to go on further. The place was most unsuitable. There was a breeze blowing downstream which created a chill factor considerably below the actual temperature; there was brush, but very little dry wood, which had to be mixed with green.

In those far off days there were no down sleeping bags as we know them today. A man had a couple of blankets or a quilt and a piece of canvas, or he took the moose hide carryall from the sides of the toboggan and used it as well. Guder held his blankets to the fire to warm them, and then rolled up in them as quickly as he could before they cooled off. Still it was too cold to get much sleep. In two days they overtook the main party, and for the next eleven days they all travelled together taking share and share alike of the toil inherent in breaking trail. Each man had a team of from five to six dogs, and usually three men went ahead on snowshoes to pack the trail for the toboggans, and the dog teams of these men were brought along by the others.

Nobody possessed such a thing as a watch or a clock. There was little or no use for such things. There were no trains to catch or appointments to keep in the hills. When the big dipper swung to a certain place in the sky it was time to get up and make ready to go. It was bitterly cold all the way. When they finally reached Pete Boxon's place on the Pelly Lakes, the mercury of his thermometer was out of sight below the minus sixty mark.

Pete, who had seen nobody since the fall, was delighted to see them, and because he had a good large building they all stayed inside for the night. He kept Guder up most of the night to satisfy his need for somebody to talk to, and when Guder finally got a chance to get to sleep it was 3:00 a.m. At 10:00 a.m. they were on the trail again for Pelly Banks—bright sunlight, still air, and the thermometer still out of sight. By the time they had reached Pelly Banks two days later the temperature had moderated somewhat, and Del VanGorder, who was the trader there for Taylor and Drury, had a thermometer which read only forty below.

This was the end of the trail for the Indians. They traded off the fur they had, picked up the ammunition they required together with a few other supplies, and were off again for the camp 150 miles back into the Nahanni Valley. Guder went on a further seventy-five miles to Ross River.

It was considerably different at Ross River at that time, compared to the way it is now. It was an isolated place in the true sense of the word. The only communication there with the ouside world was the visit of a small river boat from Whitehorse once a year with trade goods for the trading post. This was the only occasion when there was an arrival of mail, unless in a very isolated instance somebody made the trip across country with dogs from Carmacks. Then one might expect some letters apart from the river boat visit. There were possibly half a dozen white people in the whole area, plus, of course, the Indians who were most generally on the move between the various camps where they fished, hunted, trapped, or picked berries, according to the season.

In July when the boat came, the trappers had been drifting toward the focal point. There was little to be purchased before the arrival of the boat to fill the place with supplies for another year, but there was visiting to be done. This was the only social intercourse these people had with others of their kind, that time when they converged on Ross River Post for the visit of the boat. There was a little bit to drink, there were some fairly high stake poker games, and there might even have been some sort of a dance. When the visiting was done, they traded off the fur they had brought in, picked up the supplies they required, and headed back to the trap lines or other areas of endeavour. It is hard to realize that there were no radios or telephones—just moccasin telegraph.

The Pelly River was officially discovered by Robert Campbell, one of a group of intrepid Hudson Bay officers who, in their zeal to expand the trading facilities of the Company, have been responsible for the exploration and the opening up of the great Canadian northwest. The early day travellers held mostly to the waterways, and Robert Campbell having made his way up the Liard followed one of the larger tributaries in a northerly direction, and discovered Frances Lake in 1840. He named it for the wife of Sir George Simpson, the Governor of the Hudson Bay Company. He continued northerly on what is known as the Yusezyu River, crossed a height of land and found himself on the head waters of the Pelly and the Yukon watershed, as opposed to the Liard and MacKenzie drainage system. This river he named for one of the Governors of the Company, Sir Henry Pelly. In 1842 he established a trading post at Pelly Banks, thirty some odd miles above Hoole Canyon, and the following year while descending the Pelly discovered Ross River, which he named for Duncan Ross, the then Chief Factor of the Company.

Subsequently he arrived at the mouth of the Pelly, and named the large river that the Pelly empties into after another Chief Factor of the Company, John Lee Lewes. This river, which is actually the main body of the Yukon watershed was known as the Lewes River from the mouth of the Pelly to the south to its origins in the large string of lakes that cluster about the British Columbia—Yukon border. From the Pelly downstream the river always has been known as the Yukon, having been discovered, ascended and named from its mouth in the Bering Sea. In 1954 that part of the river known as the Lewes was officially renamed Yukon, so that the fabulous river now carries its name from source to mouth.

In those early days, Robert Campbell also established trading posts at Frances Lake, and one at the mouth of the Pelly which he named Fort Selkirk. The Pelly Banks trading post burned in 1850, and along with the Frances Lake post was abandoned as being considered too dangerous and too expensive to keep up. Fort Selkirk was likewise abandoned after it had been attacked and pillaged by the Chilkat Indians on August 21, 1852. Fort Selkirk was eventually rebuilt across the river from the original site.

It flourished as a trading post, riverboat stop, Mounted Police detachment, and focal point for many years until the advent of roads in the north and the discontinuance of the colourful river boats. Now it stands empty again.

In his book, *Through The Sub-Arctic Forest,* Warburton Pike makes no mention of a settlement or post at the mouth of the Ross River in the year 1887, when he sojourned down the Pelly from its upper reaches. So far as can be ascertained, the first building at Ross River was a trading post established by Tom Smith in 1903. Later he sold out to a Mr. Lewis, who named his trading post "Nahanni House". It was known as Nahanni House in the year 1905 when Charles Sheldon visited and wrote about it in his book, "The Wilderness of the Upper Yukon".

He mentions meeting Ira VanBibber at that time. He notes him as "a stalwart fellow brought up in the mountains of Kentucky", and says that he "was there to meet his partner Van Gorda (he spells it incorrectly) and with him was a young Indian boy from Liard Post. These two men had wintered in the vicinity of Pelly Lakes and planned to return there."

By the time Guder arrived back in 1919 from the Nahanni, it was known as Ross River, and there were two stores—one on each side of the river. The one store was operated by Taylor and Drury Ltd., a pioneer Whitehorse firm that operated trading posts throughout the southern part of the Territory; and the other was run by Tom Bee, a former Taylor and Drury employee from the village of Carmacks.

The first Royal Northwest Mounted Police officer to be stationed there was Jack MacDonald, who had arrived and set up shop during the interval that Guder was away in the valley. They met for the first time when Guder arrived from Pelly Banks that winter. Jack MacDonald was a devotee of boxing, had brought some boxing gloves with him, and so invited Guder across the river for the evening to do some boxing.

Guder felt he would prefer first to see an exhibition of the manly art before he decided to try his skill. Accordingly, the Swedish storekeeper obliged, and he and MacDonald put the gloves on for a round or two. Guder noticed that MacDonald was fast and knowledgeable, and that the storekeeper, who was a big man and outweighed MacDonald by a least thirty pounds, was covering up most of the time.

It didn't take Guder long to figure out that all he was going to be required to do was let loose with a Sunday punch on Jack MacDonald's chin and that would be that. The difficulty was, when he finally got the gloves on and had sparred around a little and then went for MacDonald's chin, all he hit was thin air. Jack had seen it coming from away back, and had moved his chin out of the way. By way of a riposte he hit Guder a good belt on the ribs under the arm, which put him to the wall for a moment or two. The second time he went for the chin he ended up on the floor in a corner, and concluded that this was not his game. Guder visited for a day or two, and then took the trail back.

He thoroughly enjoyed his run back to the cabin deep in the Nahanni Valley, a distance of 250 miles, some odd. His dogs were well fed and rested, and he was young, fit and capable of coping with any challenge that arose out of the stimulating environment in which he found himself.

The trail, well-used now, led him up the Pelly, past Pelly Banks, up the stream to Pelly Lakes, and across country to his cache and canoe. All the way he was constrained to remember the unceasing and relentless toil that had brought him over the same route by water the previous fall.

He stayed a day with his friend, Pete Boxon, and a day at his cache to rest his dogs and load what he would need for the rest of his sojourn. Then, up and over the height of land and so down the Nahanni to his cabin and trap lines.

He had groceries again—flour, sugar, tea, beans, rice and bacon. At Pete Boxon's the two men boiled up and mashed several pots of Pete's home-grown spuds, then set them out, rolled like so many snow balls, to freeze. He also got a sack of frozen white fish, mostly for the dogs. He took some comfort from the thought of the good load of dried moose meat on the roof of his cabin. A nice feeling, because he knew that there would be small likelihood of shooting more moose at this time of year when they usually migrate out to lower altitudes where the snow is not so deep.

Such a man at such a time is no less than king. In all his days he would remember the exhilaration he experienced during the time it took him to return to the valley. He felt no stranger in the primeval forest or the vast open spaces through which he moved now with a sure and familiar tread. He revelled in his strength and vigour, and was stirred to the utmost by the magnificence of the mountains and the long vistas that occasionally opened to his view as he crossed the height of land and made his way along the trail down the east slope into the valley.

He travelled through crisp, sunny days, spending long stimulating hours on the trail. There were cold, clear, starlit nights when he slept a restful, rejuvenating sleep close by his dogs, each curled on a little pile of boughs and each with a belly full of fish, and a slab of crusted snow stood on edge behind for a windbreak.

The mixture of wood smoke and tobacco smoke that assailed his nostrils was ever so pleasant to his senses as he relaxed by the fire each night before giving himself over to sleep. Each day and each night he renewed the pleasures and delights of the previous day and night, and before he knew it he was back again at the little cabin.

The Indians had gone from their camp across the stream, and he discovered with some consternation that his supply of dried moose meat was gone as well. There was a remote chance of there still being the odd moose that had not moved out yet, so the following morning he set out to see if this was or was not the case. He figured to travel upstream on one of the creeks, considering that if there were indeed any moose left he would have a better chance of meeting it than if he moved down river behind. His thinking was good in this instance. He ran into three moose in a bunch and shot them all.

For the remainder of the winter he busied himself collecting fur. The wolverine were thick in the area, and he managed to catch a few despite their propensity to be clever and rapacious. Most trappers consider if there is a particularly sagacious wolverine on the trap line that cannot be caught, there is little to do but move to another area. They have been known to follow a trapper, spring the traps, eat the bait, and generally put his efforts to no avail.

It was still bitterly cold most of the time, but now each succeeding day was a little longer, and Guder knew the time was in the offing when he must start back toward his cache on the height of land. If he timed it right he would have good snow to travel his toboggan on, and not too long to wait for the ice to go out of the river so he could bring out his canoe.

Soon the time came when he left his cabin for the last time and said goodbye, in effect, to the Nahanni Valley, and made his way with his dogs and furs and the last of his supplies back to the cache and to his canoe. When he arrived the river was still ice, so he made his way on down to the Pelly Lake and visited with his friend, Pete Boxon, for awhile before going back again to put in the time trapping beaver. Spring is the time for beaver, so he filled his days in this wise while he waited.

Spring is a pleasant time of year, and as Guder waited for the ice to go from the stream he had time to watch the process of the winter losing its grip and taking with it as it retired the cold, the snow, and the silence. Each day the sun rose earlier and a little farther to the north on the horizon, and each day it set a little later and at a point a little farther to the north on the western horizon. With the gradual lengthening of the days the air became warmer, and with the warmer air came life, quickened again for another cycle.

One by one the birds began to return, and the squirrels to fill the woods again with their chatter, and soon the stream opened in the centre and once the water broke free it rapidly cut away the ice and the stream was open. Ice and snow still slung to the side along the banks, as if reluctant to leave, but it was just a matter of time before the freshet really started. Guder left long before the full force of the run-off, and as a consequence of this he traversed without difficulty the dangerous places he had noted on the way upstream. The only time that he, his canoe and his possessions were endangered was when his dogs all left one side of the canoe at once to take after a moose on the bank. He jumped for the other side and kept his craft from capsizing, and thereafter kept his dogs close chained to a long pole down the centre of the canoe on the bottom.

At Wolf Canyon he pulled his canoe across the portage with the dogs, and between them they packed the rest of this stuff on their backs. At Hoole Rapids he rode through with no serious difficulty, and met a Frenchman at Hoole Canyon who helped him pack the canoe on the portage there. Guder liked this Frenchman, and was sorry subsequently to learn of his disappearance, and of how his dogs chewed through the cabin door to free themselves when he did not return. Two years went by before his body was found where there had been a snow slide.

And so Guder came again to Ross River with his canoe, his dogs, his fur, and his gear, and brought to an end his adventurous trip into the fabulous Nahanni Valley during the winter of 1918-19.

Harry Gordon-Cooper was born in Calgary, Alberta in 1912. At an early age he displayed a taste for adventure by going to sea at 17. He left the sea after two years in order to improve his education, and returned to find suitable employment and live in Hong Kong. These were the Depression years and when he found it impossible to implement his plans he, like many others of his generation, worked where he could. He accumulated four years experience as a physical-education and gymnastic instructor, plus 4 years training as a dancer. He had decided this was to be his profession, but when the war came, joined the R.C.A.F instead. He served as a pilot attached to the R.A.F. and finished the war as a Flight Lieutenant with a Mention in Dispatches.

Harry arrived in the Yukon in 1947. As a bush pilot, hydrometric surveyor, camp cook, horse wrangler, prospector, and, for a time, Clerk of the Police Magistrate's Court, he travelled his adopted territory and knew most of the lakes and rivers, and the old-timers who lived by them, before roads replaced waterways as traffic routes. He has been keeping notes for decades on these stories which are part of the fabric of Yukon history—of a period largely lost or just plain ignored, between the Gold Rush and the current 'boom' which began in the 1950's. Most of the stories come from his early days as a bush pilot, and although he lives in Whitehorse today, he maintains that "as with most northerners," he tries to spend as much time in the bush as possible. Possibly that is no longer true of most northerners, but at least, the author feels, they can still enjoy reading about the days when it was. "I wanted to write down and perpetuate their stories before they were lost," explains Harry Gordon-Cooper—Yukoner.